# Storyteller

## CHARLIE LANDSBOROUGH

# Storyteller

Trinity Mirror NW²

'Storyteller – The Autobiography of Charlie Landsborough'
is published by

# Trinity Mirror NW²

Trinity Mirror North West & North Wales
PO Box 48
Old Hall Street
Liverpool L69 3EB

Business Development Director:
Mark Dickinson

Business Development Executive Editor:
Ken Rogers

Written by:
Charlie Landsborough

'Storyteller' Book Editor:
Peter Grant

'Storyteller' Assistant Book Editor:
Vicky Andrews

Design/production:
Zoë Bevan

Cover Design:
Glen Hind

Images courtesy of:
Charlie Landsborough

ISBN 9 781906 802059

*This book is dedicated to my Mam and Dad,
and to Thelma*

# Contents

# A Foreword by Daniel O' Donnell

---

THERE are many entertainers who are incredibly talented.

Among this group, there are a few who touch people's lives in an extraordinary way.

Charlie Landsborough is one of these special entertainers.

He has a God given gift to write songs with a message that reaches the very soul of the listener.

To meet Charlie is always a joy for me. His calmness brings something special to any company he graces.

Being from Liverpool, he can't avoid having that unique sense of humour that Liverpudlians are famous for.

This book will give those of you who are not lucky enough to know him personally, a chance to meet a true gentleman.

*Daniel O' Donnell*

2009

# Five Words

Ricky Tomlinson
Author, comedian, star of stage and screen

CHARLIE Landsborough is another of those singing sensations who found 'overnight success' and stardom in only just under 30 years.

Playing in pubs and clubs, Charlie has always been true to his roots and his own wonderful style of songs and singing.

His lyrics are profound and meaningful and had Charlie not become the star we know and love he may well have become the Poet Laureate. I have seen and heard him play many times, from tiny venues to the impressive Liverpool Philharmonic Hall, and I am always inspired by his warmth, wit and sincerity. His rapport with his audience is a joy to be hold.

Classical singers are trained to sing in a particular way, their voices emanting from lungs and throat, while Charlie has perfected his own method of singing from his heart. His songs are of people and emotions and hope – things we all share.

I have many favourite songs from Charlie's vast repertoire and I love to listen to them as I drive thousands of miles to and from different locations doing my work – it's a sure way to combat road rage. Charlie Landsborough is my friend, a forever friend and I feel very proud and privileged to know him, to share the odd drink and joke with him. I also greatly admire his strength in his faith – yet another example to us all. God bless you Charlie and please God, may you carry on entertaining us all with your wonderful words and music.

## George Hamilton IV
### The man behind the hits *Abilene* and *Canadian Pacific*

I WAS at a Willie Nelson concert in Nashville and I heard him referred to as a 'modern day Shakespeare'.

The thought occurred to me that there's one in Shakespeare's own country, too, and his name is Charlie Landsborough. I don't know who the current Poet Laureate is but I'd like to nominate Charlie as the next one.

In my opinion he certainly qualifies. I'm a Charlie Landsborough fan and I am honoured, privileged and richly blessed to be a friend of his.

May God bless you Charlie and may you stay 'Forever Young'.


## Gerry Marsden
### Gerry & The Pacemakers

I'VE followed Charlie's career and his amazing catalogue of awards which says a lot about the man.

Charlie has a rare gift – a very talented artist and a really great fella, he sings from the heart and writes music from his experiences.

What more could you ask for?

I'll never forget the first time I saw Charlie on stage, my dad took me to see him when I was very young and I thought he was great then – joking aside, he's a dear friend of mine and my wife, Pauline.

Charlie I hope that you get everything you wish for.

Take care, Charlie – a great storyteller.

Bill Harry

Founder of Mersey Beat, author of 'Bigger Than The Beatles'

KNOWN by some as the 'Nashville of the North', the city of Liverpool once had the biggest country music scene in Europe.

It seems fitting then that Charlie Landsborough is now one of the world's leading Country performers and most of his albums have topped the British Country Music charts.

Apart from his popularity as a singer, Charlie has also found success as a songwriter, with his songs being recorded by a number of Country Artists including Jack Jones, Pat Boone, Foster and Allen, George Hamilton IV and Daniel O'Donnell.

Charlie has won just about every award possible in the UK country scene, including Single of the Year, Record of the Week, Top Solo Performer of the Year, North Country Music Song of the Year, Favourite Album, Most Popular Male Vocalist, Best Album by A British Act, Best Song By A British Songwriter, Best British Male Vocalist, International Country Music Album of the Year – and not forgetting the BBC Radio Scousology Award for Best Music and Best Personality.

He has also been nominated as the Best Global Country Artist at the Country Music Awards in Nashville.

I think that Charlie's numerous awards speak volumes about the diversity of this much loved musician.

Ken Dodd

Comedian

CHARLIE Landsborough is a gentle man and a gentleman.

He is a performer who exudes warmth on and off stage. He has a very loyal following and deserves his success across the world.

# Overture
## An Introduction

---

NOW here I am at the Grand Old Opry – the El Dorado of many a musical prospector's dreams – so many songs and experiences have led me here, and singing into a microphone with a brush handle as a mic stand seems so long ago.

For all the ups and downs along the way – the journey was well worth it for the destination, and I thank God for the wonderful musical gift that brought me here.

The trip may well have been long and scattered with disappointments and odd rejections, but it was always an adventure that has led me to many different places, and has blessed me with many wonderful people along the way.

I hope you enjoy my musical pilgrimage, and the situations and people that have coloured my life so wonderfully.

Let the story begin....

Charlie Landsborough

# 1. The Love of a Family

I WAS born on October 26th, 1941. My mother had been sent away to Wrexham to escape the bombs – I never really understood that because you were sent away from the bombs to be born but once you'd arrived you were sent back.

My mother got off the 94 bus with me in her arms, and my brother Derek met us and carried me into our house. I believe I cried all the way. And I was back in Birkenhead.

Our house was marvellous to grow up in. I was the youngest, and so I suppose I was a bit spoilt. My elder brothers would go off sailing the seven seas and they would bring me fantastic gifts back – silk jackets from Japan, carved boats from Africa, I used to pick up the guitars they'd bought in Spain and smell the wood.

I even got a monkey once – our Harry brought a monkey back from West Africa. So this house was full of life and full of animals.

We always had a cat and a dog and we had a budgie – at one time we had love birds from Africa – and we had chickens and even a duck at one stage in the back, which used to attack everyone that came in through the back door. It was a great house to be around.

The monkey came when Harry's crewmates all decided, during a visit to West Africa, that they all should have a monkey. And Harry's was named Jacko.

Now, after about two days out at sea, the captain caught wind of the fact that there were monkeys all over the ship, and the order went out – all monkeys overboard. Harry thought, "they're not getting my monkey" so to hide it from view he drugged it with a mixture of Aspirins and rum, so the poor old animal spent the whole trip drugged. By the time it arrived home in Birkenhead it was a bit of a drunk and an addict – but it kept it quiet and it kept it alive.

Things were much more lax in those days, and the customs man came on board the ship and disappeared having never found anything. As Harry was going through Ellesmere Port gates where they docked, he had this big overcoat on with huge pockets, with the drugged monkey inside, and as he was going through the lads on the dock gates shouted: "Alright, Harry, have a good leave won't you mate?" And then as he got further up the road they shouted: "And look after that monkey!" So they knew he had it all along.

That monkey was fantastic for me because it made me the most popular lad in the school – they all wanted to go and see Charlie's monkey.

I used to love it. It was a bit of a character and used to sit on mam's clothes drier and catch flies and moths. It would take a cup of tea off me and pass it back.

I remember Mam kept the best dishes in the top cupboard, and he got up there one day and first inspected the dishes quizzically, then tossed them all around the room. Mam was quite a stout lady and she couldn't get up there to stop him.

When he first arrived, my Mam said: "You can get that thing out of here. I'm not having it living in this house." Mam was sat with my sisters, all around the room looking extremely apprehensive, with the monkey in the middle. Anyway, we did look after it.

But when he eventually died we all cried because they all grew to love him.

He was taken down the pub one night, and I know it was a terrible thing to do to bring the monkey out of its own natural habitat, but I didn't know then.

Anyway, he was down the pub and he picked out the winning Spot The Ball ticket and I think they won twenty three pounds, which was a lot of money then, and they all came back drunk including the monkey.

My Dad used to take bets, when it wasn't legal to do so. People used to be coming to the back door to hand in their bets, and a dog got in the back yard. Now, we had our own dog, which the monkey used to enjoy riding about on while the dog just looked resigned.

So when this other dog came into the yard, the monkey jumped on it, and I've never seen a dog look so terrified, and it tore off howling, but it never ventured again into our back yard.

But the main feature of our house was the music. And I can remember, before I ever learned to play the guitar, sitting with an old tin, banging it like a drum while the rest of the family played and sang, and it was that moment I realised that music transported you from the everyday world and carried you off to another place, and I liked that place. I would sit in the corner of a house full of music and laughter, and soak it all in.

My brother Arthur used to sleep in the same room as me, and he was a naturally generous character who would give anything to anyone – he would continue to look after me on and off for a long time. He used to sail on convoys across the Atlantic, when he was fifteen, and he didn't used to talk much about it unless he'd had a bit of a drink. Then he'd tell me little stories about how ships close to him would be blown out of the water, and how they knew U boats would be close by and they'd wonder if they'd be next.

You can imagine how terrifying it must have been for a fifteen-year-old. He had some awful experiences, and some funny ones.

It was not usual for the Merchant Navy to allocate two brothers to the same ship, but my brothers, Arthur and Jack, had different names. Mam had married twice – her first husband had drowned in the dock, so there were Englands, and Landsboroughs in our family.

So Arthur and Jack ended up sailing on the same ship to New Zealand, Arthur loved it and told Jack he was jumping ship and staying. But Jack wanted to stay as well, and Arthur knew that this would break their Mam's heart, so they both decided to stay on the ship and come home. But Arthur always said that if he could ever live anywhere else it would be New Zealand.

When Arthur got into the stages of Alzheimer's, his wife Theresa took him to the doctor who started to ask him gentle questions to test his memory. He asked him where he last lived, what his last job was, that sort of thing, and sadly Arthur couldn't remember anything. So the doctor said: "Don't worry about it Arthur, you've just got a touch of . . . erm . . . a touch of . . . ermmm" and Arthur said, "You're as bad as I am." He hadn't lost his sense of humour completely.

But when it did take its hold on him I had the task of taking him to the retirement home – there was no way his wife could look after him safely.

I remember taking him to the home in Upton, not far from Birkenhead, and we went in the room and he whispered to me: "We'll be alright here, there's a window we can get out of." He was looking at it like it was a prisoner of war camp, and it was heartbreaking to leave him looking out of the window.

It was a relief actually when he did go because the Arthur that we knew and loved had disappeared.

So that's a little insight into my brother Arthur, who looked after everyone and who with Jack of course, started me playing the guitar.

I knew Arthur probably the best out of all my brothers because the others all married and left home before him, so he was the one I was most around. My brother Harry had a bad stutter, which came about after he was attacked in France during World War II – I've still got the card that came written in pencil – when almost all of his regiment was wiped out.

His pal Jimmy Clarke ended up with a plate in his head and Harry was left with a stutter. When he came home, he'd sit in front of the fire turning this picture of his regiment, which was a local one, over and over until one time when he ripped it up and threw it in the fire, and that was when he began his recovery.

But he had a hard time. I was told that a woman called to our house some time after and asked for Harry England's mother. And when Mam went out to her she said that she wanted to tell her that if it hadn't been for Harry, her son wouldn't have been alive.

Her son had been injured in the field, and Harry ran out to him and carried him out. Unfortunately the poor lad also got shot in the buttocks as Harry was carrying him, but his life was saved by Harry.

He could be a bit volatile, probably because of his experiences in the war, and Mam would always hide the knives – I never saw him use any in temper, but she did it anyway. He learned how to cook from Mam, and went off to sea ending up as a very good chef.

One time when he was working at Vauxhall he was being tailed too closely by the guy driving behind him, and this began to get on his nerves. So he suddenly braked and got out of the car to confront the guy. Now the man was smoking a pipe at the wheel and before he had a chance to do anything Harry had knocked the pipe into his throat. Not a very nice thing to do, but he was volatile – very honest and straight with you, but volatile. But I loved him to bits.

My brother Derek was only small and a bit of a Del Boy character, but good fun and a bit cheeky.

He was the one who tried to show me how to fight, even though he was only little he could fight, and he could be a bit boisterous.

I never could fight but he taught me a couple of things. He was one of the first to get married and so he left home quite early.

He was working on a boat once that had full-sized meat carcasses on board, and Harry used to travel to work on a motorbike with a little side car.

Now he and his mate took down one of the pig carcasses, and dressed it up in a hat, scarf and overcoat, and put it on the side car and drove it home to our house.

Another time he and his mates were working in Camell Laird shipbuilders and they were bunking off for a while, which I believe was the norm, and they had a crate of ale but they didn't have anywhere to go. One of them suggested this house, and Derek went and knocked on the door and invited themselves in and had a party.

I don't think Derek knew whose house it was but he ended up sleeping there. He used to dress up with my sister's skirt on, and put on lipstick and a headscarf – he made a pretty ugly woman – and he'd taunt the dockers – completely mad.

When he first went to Canada – he was in his forties then – he got a foreman's job on the dock. He could always stand up for himself and he was getting a lot of stick from a big Canadian who was shouting orders at him from the top of a crane, so he climbed to the top and challenged the lad to meet him down on the dock.

They never did fight I believe, but became the best of friends. He became a Canadian national in the end. He became a very good golfer, and footballer for that matter, and ended up calling a meeting in the golf club which he said was to decide how to, "stop these limey b******s from getting in our club." That was his character – he was game for anything.

Jack was the youngest of my brothers – he was a Landsborough whereas the others were Engands. The Englands were shorter and stockier while the Landsboroughs, like me, are taller and lankier.

Jack walked with a bit of a sailor's gait but that came about from when he was lad always climbing, and he scratched his leg and it became infected to the point of nearly having to have it amputated.

It was only due to the efforts of a German doctor that he kept his leg and was able to walk, albeit with a swagger. He sailed with the Blue Funnel Line, as did my other brothers, and I think he was one of the youngest Bosuns. He loved the sea and he could do marvellous things with ropes, and could do ships in bottles. He was quite artistic in his own way, and of course he played the guitar with Arthur.

He taught me *Deep In The Heart Of Texas* and started me off on the guitar that was to become my friend for life. Some might say he has a lot to answer for.

When the time came when my Mam was very ill, the family were hard up and Jack had a ship to go to. But he didn't want to go with Mam being so bad, but we needed the money so he went.

She passed away while he was at sea, and when he came home he bought all these gifts for my mam, and she was laid out in the front room. It was horrible for him. Like the rest of us he loved her to bits.

When she was very ill, mam couldn't leave the bedroom.

I remember reading in the paper about a 'Weeping Madonna' found in Italy I think, and the tears of this religious icon were healing people, and I thought, well I can't get to Italy, but if I cried, would the good Lord take my tears and use them in the same way to heal my Mam?

I really wanted to do it, but I was afraid if – when I went in – she would wake up and maybe laugh at me. I never did it, but to this day I think I should have done, because I think the god Lord would have taken the simplicity of a child and done the trick.

But it was not to be. I've still got a card from her for my birthday, sent when she was in hospital, and I have a letter that she wrote – it must have been so hard for her – where at the bottom it says: "Look after Charlie for me."

It was hard for us but it must have been awful for her. I got the horrible job of telling the rest of the relatives, like my Aunty, and everywhere I went I started crying as soon as I told them the news.

My mam was an absolute smasher – she had a hard life losing her first husband and two of the eleven kids she had between the two marriages, but she always seemed happy – always singing.

There was a murder in Birkenhead when I was only a kid – the Pill Box Murder – I don't think it was ever solved actually. A woman had been found murdered in a pill box on the banks of the Mersey.

(A pill box, by the way, was a very small concrete fort used as a line of defence during the Second World War.)

Anyway, I'd read about this and on the dark nights you'd find yourself thinking, I wonder if this fella's still around, you know?

My Mam used to go once a week to see my Aunty Iris – only about a mile walk away – and I was worried to death about this.

I followed her from a distance all the way to Iris's and I stood in the shadows of a block of flats all the time Mam was in there – until hours later Mam came out, and then I followed her all the way back home.

I don't know what I could have done if the Pill Box murderer had set his sights on her because I was only a little lad – but that was how much I loved my mam.

I had four sisters – Sylvia, Joyce, Doreen and Dot. I love all my family but I seem to have more memories of my brothers, probably because I was always looking up to them, being a lad.

Joyce, Doreen and Sylvia were pretty close in age and all grew up together and I believe they used to fight like cat and dog over different things, in fact when they were young Mam couldn't afford to buy three bikes, so she bought one between them. They only had it a week, there was that much fighting over it Mam took it back.

I remember poor Joyce getting a good hiding because she shut the door on me when I was sitting on the front step, and it trapped my bum and pinched it.

And of course I was the blue eyed boy with me being the youngest. I had a pair of boxing gloves and used to tease her and hit her with the gloves and she'd run off to Mam. But she had a heart of gold, as have all my sisters. Derek used to call her Snacker – I don't why, maybe she was always nibbling things I don't know.

But she was smashing.

Sylvia was a little bit deaf, but she sails through life as if there's nothing to worry her at all. In fact I don't think I've ever heard her say anything bad about anybody.

She's amazing like that, and there was a stage when she used to drive me up the wall, probably because she had this relaxed attitude to everything, it used to irritate me for some reason.

Around about the time when I was being a bit of an idiot and started getting into trouble, Sylvia was working in Cadbury's or somewhere, and she wasn't making very much money at all.

She would come around and I couldn't stand her at this time – for no good reason because she's lovely – and she used to stick a ten bob note in front of me, saying nothing, and leave me with it.

I just used to pick it up, and I never said anything, not even thank you, I'm ashamed to say. My family never ever turned on me or had a go at me, no matter what I did, when they had every right to.

Doreen was much the same, and is now living in America. When I was a lad, like most teenagers I used to get blackheads, and Doreen used to get great delight out of squeezing them for me. I looked like I'd had an attack of the plague afterwards. But she was another one who would look after me.

All my sisters married smashing lads, Sylvia married Peter Richards and Joyce married Ken – his dad, Norman, was a very good friend to me. Doreen married a Birkenhead lad and went off to America although I don't think that lasted very long.

Dot was the oldest and she was like a second mother to me. I would send her Mother's Day cards. She didn't have much of a life because she was always looking after everybody else.

I remember when I got a few bob I said to her and her husband Jim to go and have a holiday somewhere, but she was too ill by then to go. But I love my family very much – all my sisters and all my brothers.

I remember working in Ellesmere Port and standing on the line hearing this fella talking about families and how he couldn't stand his brother, and I had to tell him how much I loved my family and I thought how lucky I am to have that.

# 2. Jailhouse Rock

I WENT off the rails when I was only a lad. My mother died when I was about twelve, and that was like the centre of my world disappeared, because I loved my mum.

And then my dad died when I was eighteen. But in between, once my mum had gone and the family started disappearing, I became disenchanted after leaving school and finding that I had nothing going for me.

There were influential lads in that area – some rough characters and some dodgy characters. There were some nice ones though, but to be accepted in that locality it seemed that you had to be a fighter or a thief – and I can't fight to save my life. I've always stood up for myself but I can't really fight, although I had a go at both, to my great shame.

I suppose I wanted to be accepted by the family of my peers around the area, and I started doing petty thieving, things like breaking into picture houses, an old Co-op, silly things like that, robbing ciggies and bottles of whisky and stuff – anything.

I think it was just for excitement and a cry for attention – I'm certainly not making excuses for what I did.

I remember we were in Conway Street, and sometimes I think it was a wonder we weren't collared right there and then. There was a big glass window, and there was a little window at the top of this great frontage. I stood on top of a lad's shoulders and walked along until I got by this window and climbed through and passed all the stuff out. I had a bit of a job climbing back again, but I managed it.

And we hid the stuff in the park under the cricket pavilion. It was daft things like that.

It was a whole series of things. I was caught once, and they let me out and I did something else the following night, and when they caught me that time they put me in the Town Hall, under the clock there. It wasn't funny because I was there for a couple of days and there's nothing more boring than being in a little room and hearing that clock tolling away every quarter and every half hour and so on.

Of a night time you'd hear some sort of a noise and you'd hear people being hauled in, and some of them you knew. Eventually they moved me to Walton jail, where I spent two months sewing mail bags which I found hilarious, because I thought that was only something you saw on gangster movies. But we were sewing the mail bags – there had to be eight stitches to the inch or something – and you got a pittance for each one you sewed. In fact in the two months that I was there I think I earned one and ten in old money.

So I'd never have made a living doing it.

It was all a bit of a lesson to me. I remember my brother Derek coming up, who was a bit of a character, and he was talking to me through the grill, or whatever it was, and he said: "You want to watch your step in here, Charl." I said: "Why is that?"

He said: "They're all thieves." I could have strangled him if I'd have got hold of him.

I was in there for a while and didn't like it at all. And I missed my guitar as well. My family was very upright and very honest and had never done anything wrong, and they were aghast that 'Our Charlie' had done something wrong like I'd done.

Eventually, after a couple of months, they took me to the quarter session of Birkenhead, and I was worried to death. I thought they may give me Borstal or something, and I'll be gone for a couple of years, and I'll never see my guitar for ages, or my family.

Well on the way there it was funny, because we went on this bus, and I was handcuffed to one of these warders, and two songs came on the radio – one was very appropriate, it was Elvis Presley singing *Don't*, and the other was one that I hoped wasn't symptomatic of what was going to happen to me, Ella Fitzgerald singing *Every Time We Say Goodbye*.

But thankfully I got off. They put me on probation for a couple of years and later I'd talk to the younger lads in the area and tell them: "Don't be swallowed up by all this rubbish going on around here. Stay away from it – it's not worth it."

So it did me a lot of good but I was very much ashamed later to think back on it, but I don't think any harm came out of it.

I remember when I was in the town, when me and Thelma were courting and there was a lot of yobbos for want of a better word, as well as a lot of older people in this pub – it was a nice quiet little boozer. And this gang were there and every time an older fella would go by to go to the toilet they'd try to ridicule him or belittle him: "Where are you goin' pop? Who are you pushing?"

They did this for ages and in the end I really couldn't take it any more and I got up, stupidly and I went to the toilet.

I didn't want to go at the time but I got up, and as I did this bloke stood in my way and I just pushed him and he said: "Who are you pushing?" I said: "I'm pushing you," because I was fed up with them picking on the older fellas. And before I could do anything, the others grabbed me from behind and they gave me a bit of a hiding and cut my eye. The police came, but they all cleared off and I think the people in there knew who these lads were but they wouldn't tell the cops who they were and I was disgusted.

I said: "I've just got a good hiding for you lot and you won't even tell them who it was." They took me to hospital and what added insult to injury was when I got there with this cut over my eye, they obviously thought I was a trouble maker and a nuisance and the nurse was telling me off. So I said: "Hey love, I got this trying to help somebody – I didn't cause trouble."

It was quite funny because when these lads jumped on me they had some girls with them, but Thelma jumped on the back of one of the lads trying to stop them. She was ok though. I was incensed by all this and I didn't like these lads anyway.

I was in a pub one night, and I thought: "I'll get even with these lads." I remember I was with the next door neighbour – Monk Wallace – and I saw one of these blokes sat with a group of other lads, and among them were a couple of a particular family.

They were hard cases from round our way, especially Jake, and this lad saw me watching him and he got up to leave. I never said anything to Monk, I just followed him out. I took an empty bottle of Guinness with me. I thought he might have told the others to follow me, and I thought I'm not going to get battered by another crowd.

I'd fight him fairly – solo. He was walking on his own and he was quite a way off and I was running on tiptoes trying to get to him.

When I got close I swung a punch but he'd heard me and he ducked, and hared off up the road and I was calling him all the cowards under the sun and yelling for him to come back and fight.

But obviously he was not – he was going back to the pub for re-enforcements. I was very angry and mad, and I think back now you know, how dangerous it was what I did.

I took this Guinness bottle and hurled it and it hit him on the neck, and cut his neck open. If I'd have hit him on the head I could have killed him.

Thank God I didn't do that. He dashed into the pub and I shot by and hid over the road in the alley way, by the Empire cinema. All these lads came out to see who this phantom bottle-thrower was – Big Jake and Gerry and the other lads that were with them, and this fella with blood all over his neck. They were looking round, and I said a little prayer, which sounds a bit contradictory to say a little prayer after I've just hurt someone, but I said: "Look after me, Lord" and I walked over to the corner. And Big Jake said to me: "Where's Monk?"

I said: "It's nothing to do with Monk. It was ME."

And there was a crowd of them round me. But I said: "You don't know what happened, five or six of them jumped me the other week. I just wanted to have a go with him on my own."

Jake swung a punch at me and I dodged it, and he swung another one and I dodged that and I thought: "If he hits me I'll have to fight back and there's a crowd of them and I'll get battered."

Anyway, Gerry stepped in who was about my age and he said "Leave him Jake, leave him. Go on Charl." So I left. And I went in and got Monk Wallace who was unaware that any of this had happened, and I said: "Come on, we're going." But Jake had said: "I'll get you tomorrow."

He lived up our way so I thought if he's going to get me I may as well get it over with. He used to drink in the Rose and Shamrock up the north end of Birkenhead, so I went up to the pub early and I sat there all night waiting for Jake to come in. He came in about half past nine at night and he just walked past me and he said: "Hello Charl," and I said "Hello Jake," and he went and sat down. I could have laughed with relief. And that was it. He never did anything to me and I was so relieved. I was terrified, I thought I was definitely in for a big hiding.

During my bout of petty thieving, we had a lovely dog called Rex – a Labrador – and he had his own kennel in the back garden, well back yard really. At night Rex slept in the house. I used to hide my stolen bootie in the back of the kennel – a bottle of whisky, different bits and pieces, rubbish really. And my sister-in-law Pauline used to lock me out – she had good reason to, I was a nuisance at the time.

Sometimes I could get in through the front window if you kept pushing it and shoving it. Eventually the handle would slide down and I'd manage to get in, and close it again. And in the morning when I was lying on the couch she'd come down with a face like thunder, wondering how I'd got there.

But this one night I couldn't get in, and if it was raining when I couldn't get in I'd sleep in the dog's kennel. Rex was in the house and I'm sleeping in the kennel! Of course because of the length of me, if it was raining I'd be wet from the knees down. It was very uncomfortable.

I recall one day, Pauline was in the back kitchen looking out into the yard. The dog goes into his kennel, and comes out with a box of Black Magic chocolates in his mouth, with the cellophane still on.

Now you would always get bits of rubbish floating around the yard, but Pauline thought: "That looks new."

So the dog had a chew of that then he goes back in and comes out with a box of Bic Biro pens.

Pauline went out then and discovered my cache. Now I loved that dog but I had a little go at him and said: "You lousy thing, after the way I give you chocolates and everything." But he uncovered my cache and I don't think my problem was solved until they caught me and stuck me in Walton for that couple of months.

# 3. First Love, First Home

AH, fallin' in – and stayin' in love. Can't beat it.

When we were lads standing on the corner of Tees Street, in Birkenhead, this family moved in just down the road and a lovely girl kept passing on her way to Chester.

I thought, she would never consort with the likes of us – 'riff raff' on the corner.

Why? Because we'd all just stand there. I'd wonder where she was going all the time. She was, of course, going to Chester and didn't have anything to do with us round there.

I really fancied her, you know, and in fact she had started working as a machinist in Harella, a dress-making place, just down from where I lived in Beaufort Road.

I was very keen. I knew what time she got out each day and I would dash home to put on my one decent set of clothes – and I'd smarten myself up and stand on the corner by the pub and watch till she passed. I never spoke to her or anything that bold. I don't know what I was expecting – she certainly wasn't going to stop and speak to me. So I just fancied her from afar for a long time.

The decision time came one night when I decided to approach her. She was coming home and I'd got off the bus at the top of the hill, close to where we lived. It was getting late, well, about half past ten, and I followed her down the hill and I thought, "Charlie, here goes . . . " and I went up to her. She was still terrified, obviously, but I said: "Listen, just because I'm from around here doesn't mean to say that I'm a scoundrel or anything like that, but what's the chance . . . ?"

Still terrified, she shot off home. I kept thinking about her and still fancied her madly even if my chatting up technique needed a lot to be desired.

Years later, after I'd joined the army, I was home on leave. I was dressed in the German fashion, which, I suppose, made me look a little bit different. I was in a club down town called the Starboard Light with my brother-in-law, Peter Richards, and over the other side of the room was . . . Thelma (Cue sweeping strings and appropriate love theme music.)

Now I hate dancing – I can't do a good move on the dancefloor to save my life, but I thought I'd get up and ask her for a dance. So I did, and we did. I asked her if I could see her again and she said "YES" (Cheers of 'hooray' from readers, please!)

So we made arrangements to meet near to the Ritz Cinema in Birkenhead a couple of nights later. I got there, before the suggested time, and I stood in a shop doorway. I thought, I'm not going to stand out, I'll wait and see where she is first and make sure she comes.

So I'm standing in the doorway and NOT where I said I would be. I can picture it now. The bus arrived with her on it, and she's standing on the platform waiting to get off, and she's looking around and couldn't see me, so she went back on the bus. The bus took off, so I had to go haring after it, jump up on to it, announce my presence and ask her why she didn't get off? And she said: "Well, you weren't there," which I wasn't so to speak. So that was how we started off.

On the night I met her, I remember my brother-in-law, Peter, finished up absolutely blotto (great word for being drunk), but I was okay.

You know I always liked a bit of mischief – bit of a laugh. I was in a very good mood. I had this German gear on and so on the way home there was a group of girls coming along, and I said to Peter: "Listen, whenever I say something you just say 'Yah', okay?"

So, game for a laugh, he said: "Alright Charlie."

I stopped this group of girls and said: "Guten Abend" and a couple of other German phrases, and the girls said: "Oh, he's a foreigner, isn't he lovely?"

One of them said: "They don't understand you, mate." I said: "Me? Going to home – with you?" in my best German accent.

"Oh you can't come home with us, there's too many in our house already," she said. Anyway we kept passing them. I think we must have passed them about three times and each time we went by they'd be giggling saying, "There's that German fella!"

As I was talking to them, pie-eyed Peter had forgotten how to say 'Yah', so they were saying: "He's not German, he's just being stupid, him. But the other fella – he is."

Anyway, after passing them a few more times again we went in the chip shop and there were the girls in the back room. I could hear them whispering and giggling about me being German. So, seizing the opportunity, Charlie from Birkenhead walked in the back and said: "Alright girls, how's things?"

They all had big red faces 'cos they realised what they'd been saying.

It was just a bit of fun. But a couple of weeks later I was on the railway platform in Moreton and one of those girls came up to me – who I didn't recognise – and she said: "You're the German aren't you?" and we laughed. All good harmless mischief.

But, hey, that had been the night I'd met Thelma. I wasn't trying to take them home, I was just having a bit of fun. Honest.

So obviously, whenever I came home from the army I was seeing Thelma, and we'd write to each other while I was away and stuff like that.

When I demobbed myself from the army, I didn't have a job. Living with me were two lads who were on the run, Tanner Jones and Kenny Bowen, and we were all skint. Thelma would nip round in her dinner hour with food from her mother. So she was looking after us really. She'd cottoned on to a hopeless case (even then) at that particular time, and happily for me she persevered.

I do remember my cousin Stanley was always wanting me and Terry Lennon to go out playing our guitars around town, when I was supposed to be seeing Thelma. Me and Terry would play all night for nothing, or maybe an odd pint or two. But sometimes I was out when I should have been seeing Thelma.

One night I was in the Starboard Light – where I first danced with her (how can I forget it?)

The club was upstairs and there was a big basket about four foot high with flowers in it. In the hope of her forgiving me for not being out with her, I took the basket and presented it to her at her door at about eleven o'clock at night.

I don't know whatever happened to it. To this day I don't know how I got out with it past the bouncers. Anyway, Thelma just smiled wryly (I think that's the word) at me when I gave them to her.

When I'd left the army I got this call from Ron Thomas, who had been the bass player in a band I'd been in over in Germany, asking if I'd go to Dortmund to join them. I was delighted about this, but I didn't have much money. I asked Thelma to wait for me – and off I popped. I was supposed to be going to get money for us to get married. But being a well-meaning Scouser I left with nothing and I came back with nothing.

Now life would never be the same again for me and Thelma. We didn't tell anyone we were getting married, we just did it and got wed.

There was only five people in the church: Myself, Thelma, her friend Lily and her husband Eric – oh and the priest.

And that dearly beloved readers was it. I remember it so well. Beforehand, I went in the pub just up the road, all dressed up in my best gear and one of the lads came in and said: "You don't half look smart. Where are you going?" I said: "I'm going for a job down at the fibre glass place."

Well, I was going for a job alright – I was going to get married. And we celebrated our big day at Murphy's ale house in the back parlour. A few days later I went back to Germany to join the band.

Thelma was amazed and not very happy about it but I said that I'd promised the lads and couldn't let them down, and I wouldn't be there long. So I went back, but didn't stay long and came back to try – yes, try – and settle down.

Thanks to Thelma – she saved up the money – we bought our first house in Thornton Street, Birkenhead. It was only a little terraced house, costing in the region of £1,200. The mortgage was something like £12 a month – it might not even have been that. I remember saying at the time, "I can't afford that" which I know today seems ridiculous. But we moved into this little two-up and two-down with an outside toilet and we had a little kitchen built on to the back of it. But it was home for us for quite a while.

When I was there, I was playing my guitar and singing, and coming home late at night usually full of the joys of spring and no doubt a few pints of Guinness. I'd still be singing, oblivious to everything else, and sometimes revving my car . . . unfortunately.

Thelma's sister lived over the road and I sometimes woke her baby up. And Mrs Jones next door – a lovely lady – I often unintentionally upset her sleeping pattern too. But they all forgave me.

I remember one night I'd stayed out late and Thelma had locked me out. I had a little Mini parked out the front, and she wouldn't let me in. She'd locked the front door so I slept in the Mini. I turned the radio on and it said it was the coldest night of the year, whatever the year was, and I thought, that's comforting to know.

Picture the scene – a big, gangly thing like me, trying to sleep in a Mini with no sleeping bag or anything – it was freezing, and awkward. And you know how you get stiffness in your neck? Well, come the morning time I knocked on the door and there was still no answer. She wouldn't let me in.

I began by trying to shout quietly, because I didn't want the neighbours to hear, but I was quietly shouting through the letterbox: "Thelma, open the door." To which she replied, "Get knotted, go back where you've been all night!"

I'd only been in the pub singing and playing all night. But no. So then I started losing my temper and I was saying: "Listen I'm freezing, and I need a bath and I have to go to the toilet. And I'm hungry."

"No."

So then I shouted loudly and got a bit more ratty. But she wouldn't open the door. Thelma can be very stubborn. I finished up going round the back, climbing on the lean-to we had at the back of the house. We had a window in the back which was cracked anyway, and I'm standing on that lean-to to break the window to get into the house and Mrs Jones next door came out and said: "Good morning, Charlie."

I said "Good morning, Mrs Jones." And then I proceeded to break into the house. But Thelma was right. I shouldn't have stayed out late. I learned a lesson.

Our first child, Charlie was born at this time. I remember when he was only a couple of years old, he was only small and had climbed up a stepladder and was at the top of the wall leaning over to Mrs Jones's and I went out worried he was going to break his neck.

He was shouting, "Buddy! Buddy!" And there was only Mrs Jones there – she had a son called Robert, I think, but certainly not Buddy. I said: "Who's Buddy?" And he looked around and said: "Dad, there's no buddy in!" Lovely isn't it, what kids say?

In our street there was a really nice old fella that could hardly walk – I don't think he had both legs to be honest – who used to meet me every Sunday at the bottom of the road.

I used to give him a packet of ciggies – this sounds very noble of me but it wasn't really. He'd wait there for me and he used to call me Bill or something – he never called me Charlie. Anyway, one day when I was with a friend, he called me over and said: "Bill, get that down you," and handed me a miniature bottle of whisky.

Well at that time I never drank spirits, but I pretended I was delighted, thanked him and told him I'd really enjoy that. My friend couldn't believe that I had taken it off him, and he looked at me as though I was really mean, but he didn't understand that as long as the old man could give me something, when I had given him ciggies, we were friends. It meant he felt good about it and so did I. The lad I was with didn't understand that logic.

When we moved into that house in Thornton Street we found our bedroom was painted in all sorts of colours. I think the fella who'd owned it must have worked at Cammel Laird. There was a fire painted green, skirting boards were blue, something else was red – all sorts of colours. But we sorted that out. It was a happy little house for us.

It was while we were there that our Allan was born – our second lad – on my birthday too which was fantastic for me. (How could I forget his birth date?)

When I was working steadily we bought a house with a back garden for £6,800 and a little bit of a front greenery, whereas, at Thornton Street we'd only had a backyard, with nowhere for the kids to play. Yet when we took them up there, we were looking at the house and all there was in the back was just grass.

But the two lads were running around and they thought it was paradise, more space and somewhere the young lads could play.

I remember a couple of the lads from the local pub, Joe and

Jimmy, saying to me: "D'you want a lamp, Charlie?" I said yes – I envisaged one of these Victorian type things, you know, they look nice in gardens don't they? I was working at the Gas Board at this time, and when I came back, they'd brought the lamp. Oh yes. It must have been about forty foot long with a big curl on the end, like one of those modern ones.

I said if we'd have erected that they would have been calling Thelma 'Florence Nightingale'. They'd have redirected airplanes.

Anyway I had to break it up with a lump hammer and take it down to the scrap yard. So, I don't know whether they were laughing when they did that to me but my lamp was not at all as I expected it to be.

Getting about in the old heaps of cars that I had over the years was memorable. Thankfully, in Plessington Drive, there was a bit of a rise going up to the road and then there was a big hill. You could time your watch by me and my car in the morning. I'd have to push it up the drive on to the road and then round about the corner I would jump in and turn the corner and, hopefully, by the bottom of the hill it was going.

Ninety nine point nine per cent of the time it did get going, but in the bad weather I'd get all the way to the bottom of the hill and there was still NO sign of life out of it. The neighbours must have had a laugh watching me.

I once had two friends who meant well, but one of their kindly gestures certainly backfired. We had bad reception for the television, and while we were out my mates came round and said: "Let's sort that out for them." So they got up on the flat roof to sort the aerial out. A few nights later I was in the bedroom writing a song, playing into a little tape recorder, and I heard this gushing of water. When I turned around there was water pouring down inside, and pouring down outside. It was actually gushing water into this room. When my handymen had got up to repair the aerial, they'd put a big hole in the dormer roof. I never told them but I had to redirect the water. I had a paddling pool in the bedroom. We had to sleep in another room because of that. Those dormer bungalows are terrible.

At work I was driving a wagon and labouring for Johnson and Stubbs, a gas firm, and I'd also rediscovered my faith, which caused a bit of a situation. I remember being sent over to Liverpool and I pulled up at Broadgreen Hospital and there was a gang of Liverpool lads in the back who I'd never met before. I knew the lad in the front next to me – another Scouser called Pat Flannery – and when we pulled up the lads all said: "You'll be alright here lad, there's loads of wood and paint round here."

I thought I'd better get off to the right start, so I said: "Listen, lads I know you mean well, and I appreciate the thought but I can't do anything like that. I can't take anything because of my faith. I'm a Christian – I believe in Jesus Christ."

Well it was like an admission of being gay or something else that shouldn't really cause shock or offence. The silence in the back was deafening. But one by one these lads sought me out and asked me if I definitely absolutely meant what I said.

One of the lads, Stan, who used to deal in stolen goods would come round but would always ask where I was before he got the stuff out. With respect for me he wouldn't try and sell anything while I was about. He was a comical character and I liked him.

At that same time, when I was driving the wagon, I remember Cliffy Starkey asking if I could help him move house.

So I did, and the following day I went to my job on the gas board and there were a couple of articles of clothing left in the back – one of which was a pair of ladies' briefs, and of course the lads were all ready to pull my leg – "So much for Holy Joe, look what we found in here!"

But what they didn't tell me is that at the end of the day they had tied them to the van's radiator and I drove home with this pair of ladies' briefs on the front of my van. I know that didn't go down too well.

Back home I loved fatherhood and discovered what a responsibility it was. When you've got kids you sometimes notice when the house goes suddenly quiet and it sort of frightens you. One day I was home and I realised it had gone quiet – and I thought, "Where's Allan?" and there was silence and I went charging upstairs.

When I got up to the landing there were razor blades all over the floor and I thought, "Oh no," and I dashed into the room fearing the worst, and he was standing there looking a bit sheepish and a bit afraid, and he had his arms up his jumper – he was still standing thank God – and I pulled his arms out and he had little nicks all over them.

God knows how he got hold of those blades because they were in a cupboard above the sink, but he'd somehow managed to get up there and get them out. It was terrifying.

It was while we were there that one of the worst times of my life occurred. We had another little lad – we called him Roy Samuel. He was lovely. He was only a couple of months old when one night we went to bed, only to find silence when we woke in the morning. It was a cot death and they took him away.

I walked the street and cried my eyes out for what seemed an eternity. It was the most awful feeling, I wanted to die, you know, but I thought I can't do that I've got other lads here.

I went to church on the Sunday. I've always thought that day rather odd, because they don't normally use passages from the Book of Wisdom, I don't think it's in the canon according to the Protestant Church, which was the one I was attending at the time.

But on this Sunday there was a passage from the Book of Wisdom and it said things like: "He was taken before the world could corrupt him," and it was almost like the Almighty was talking to me.

So I drew some consolation from that. And with any kids – nobody's aware of this half the time, with my own kids – I'd pray over them. I'd put my hand over their head and say: "Dear Lord look after this little lad, watch over him all the days of his life, and may he turn out to be a servant of yours. Bring him to your salvation at the end of this life." And I do that with my grandkids – I don't think anybody's aware of that, other than me and the Almighty. And now you.

Thankfully, I had done this with Roy and I like to think he is safe in the arms of the Almighty. But it was an awful time for me and obviously for Thelma. I'm talking about me very selfishly, but for her it was unbelievable.

The easing of grief and pain came shortly after, when Thelma gave birth to Jamie, and I suppose if Roy had lived we wouldn't have had Jamie. So that was some form of consolation for losing one.

That hole inside you that's created by losing a child – I don't think that ever completely goes away. Sometimes when you might be feeling ok, something will remind you, and this huge chasm inside you opens up again.

It's something that never leaves you really.

# 4. Work is a Many Splendoured Thing

THE first job I got after I was married was as a labourer with the Gas Board.

The money wasn't much. One week I'm sure I worked something like 120 hours. We'd worked all through the night outside a pub on a main road, and we'd done like three weeks amount of work.

I thought to myself, what a payout I'm gonna get here. I actually got 22 pound or something like that. I know it was a long while back, but it wasn't very much then. I enjoyed the work though because you were out in the fresh air.

I started on a building site with its own gang hut, and there was about six of us and we had great fun. The 'ganger' at that time was a fella called Freddy Crane who had this wonderful knack of saying words wrongly, you know, malapropisms, and that sort of thing. He was a big lad, he was like a wrestler – so you couldn't really laugh with Freddy about what he'd said.

One morning, while we were having our tea in the shed, Freddy said he'd watched this cowboy film, and we were all bored to death listening, but he was telling us about this film and how marvellous it'd been. It came to this point and he said: "This cowboy walked through these swing doors, fired his gun and the bullet rhinocerated round the room." Now isn't that a wonderful word 'rhinocerated.'

For all the fresh air on offer, the Gas Board was pretty hard work, especially for somebody who wasn't used to that sort of manual labour, but I made the most of it and enjoyed it and was there for quite a while. Tanner Jones, who I'd been in the army with, worked with me for a short while, and Kenny Bowen, another ex-army mate both on the same job – that was a bonus. And also later, my guitar-playing mate Terry Lennon.

You know, in the old days you could get different jobs quite easily. Me and a few lads once went down to the flourmills, which were just down the road from us, and three of us landed a job.

The bloke who interviewed me took me to one side and said: "Oh you've got a bit of an education, I'll put you in such and such a section."

I thought, that's great, it must be a bit of a move up the ladder. The other two lads were just put on these trolley things, and I said to them: "I'll see you later lads at the end of the day."

So the boss put me in this department on this floor . . . cleaning – that's what my education brought me. The fella who was looking after this particular floor said: "Right, get on the top of that machine and clean it all off." Now it was obvious he hadn't done any cleaning on the top of this machine and it was thick with flour.

Well, you should have seen the state of me when I came out that day. In fact, the two lads who were waiting for me, as I walked past, didn't even know it was me. I was covered in flour from head to toe. Needless to say, I didn't last long there.

I often think back in horror to that place. They had these milling machines and I liked the feel of the flour.

In one of these contraptions there was a hole and I stuck my hand inside and this fella shrieked at me. As I stepped back he said to me: "Anyone with a grain of sense would have known there was a 'worm' device inside." He pointed out that if I'd left me hand there, I would have lost it, and maybe part of my arm as well.

So somebody up there was looking after me. There wouldn't have been any guitar playing if that had happened.

But that was the flour mills – didn't last long there – my career certainly didn't flower but at least I came away with my limbs in tact.

I once got a job with my cousin Stanley. This time on the railways, cleaning again, but it was engines. I used to cross the electric line to get to the sheds which weren't far from us. Stanley said to me out of the blue: "I've got to go to court, Charl."

He was always in trouble because of a severe drink problem, he'd do anything for a drink our Stanley.

So he had to go to court and said: "I'll see you later." Well he didn't actually come round later and his mother came around – my Aunty Kate – and said: "Have you seen Stanley?"

Well he'd already said to me: "Listen Charl, don't tell me mam," so I said: "No I haven't, Kate. He left work and I haven't seen him," which I suppose was true.

He'd said it was only some minor thing.

Well he did come back later . . . SIX months later. He'd jumped through some window when he was blotto – a quaint expression meaning out of the game, another quaint drinking expression. He was always in and out of trouble because of the drink. I don't think he remembered half of it to be honest.

Then there was another job I did for a very short space of time at a nearby fibre glass factory, where I got a start on nights. One evening I went in and I think I'd had a pint on my way in – it was a horrible place to work and you could see all the little bits of fibre glass in the air, little needles of it even got in your skin.

This fella was supposed to be showing me how to do this particular job with bobbins of fibre glass being rolled, and I said I had to go to the toilet (must have been the pint I had on my way in) and I told him I wouldn't be long. I went to the toilet and fell asleep and the next thing I heard was the buzzer to clock off.

So I went and clocked off.

When I came in the following night the fella said: "What happened to you?" And I had to make up some lie about not feeling too good. I think I only lasted a week or two at the most.

Another job I had was at the Co-op. When I was at the Gas Board, Kenny McGunigall – who played in the duo with me – got a job with the Co-op as a trainee manager and I thought: "That sounds great! That's definitely a better class of job than what I'm doing now with a shovel in my hand."

So, determined to better myself, I applied and I got a start as a trainee manager. They put me in a large Co-op in Grange Road. And I got all the dirty jobs to do.

The boss would say: "I think there's a shoplifter out on aisle three." I'd have to go out and collar them.

I believed if I was getting paid to do a job properly I had to nab or collar them – not a very pleasant thing to do. Anyway, this time I went out and peered round the corner of aisle three and it was my wife's brother's mate, Tom.

He used to have a little removals thing called Tom and Jerry. I don't know whether he was shoplifting or removing things in the store but I thought I can't grab HIM – my life would be a misery. So I just went back and said he wasn't doing anything. I've always been loyal.

I remember stacking shelves too. What a very menial type of employment and I remember the lads coming by on their way down to the pub on a Saturday afternoon, and there was me, with my white smock on, stacking tins of peas.

And there were the lads standing with sombre looks on their faces shaking their heads as if to say: "Charlie, that's NOT for you."

And it wasn't me. I was already past my sell-by date.

But I did stay there for a while enough to recall incidents, like the time someone said there was a mouse. Well, there were always a few mice.

I grabbed this one eventually – it wouldn't look good for shoppers with this rodent running around the shop. I carried it out to the back and over to the wasteland. I couldn't kill it, you know, just couldn't.

Anyway, I think the mouse was back in the shop before I was.

They even sent me on a training course and then moved me to this other Co-op to manage it.

The stress of that job was unbelievable. By this time I'd found my Faith and naturally I wouldn't steal anything – not a bent tin of peas or anything.

To keep the place ticking over I was staying there until very late some nights. I was attempting to bring goods in at the back, sign for them, check them, stack the shelves, run to the tills, catch shoplifters – all sorts of things connected with running a store. It was very, very stressful.

One day a big boss came in – he wasn't that old – and he started saying something to me about the shop. I just didn't like his attitude.

I asked if we could go into the office away from prying eyes and ears and once inside said: "Listen, before we go any further, speak very carefully to me and speak politely and I'll speak politely to you. Because if you don't I don't know what's liable to happen with the week I've just had."

Both fridges had gone off and everything seemed to have gone wrong. And I was trying to do it all on my own.

He told me I'd have to come with him to the head office, and I knew if I went I wouldn't come back. So I got my coat and I got a couple of cakes (I'd got off one of the tradesmen) and I gave them to the shop girls. When they said: "Where are you going, Charlie?" I said: "Ta ra, I'll see you sometime."

When we got in the car I said: "When we get to these bosses don't think that because you're in the company of them you can start mouthing off because I'm liable to explode."

Anyway, we got down there and they started to tell me off and I said: "Listen keep the job," (I probably never said it in such a polite way, though, dear reader).

I added: "You don't know what you've lost. I'm very honest. I've worked all hours and what superman are you going to get in to replace me?"

In fact I met the girls from work some weeks later and they said they had two blokes in there following my departure and they couldn't do it. When I got home to Thelma I told her I'd packed in yet another job. But I was glad. I was so relieved I'd left that job. Stress-free for a while.

I also once signed up for Vauxhall where two of my brothers worked – Harry and Arthur. I got a job on the gearbox line, which is probably the worst section to be on. So I got the worst job on the worst line. I couldn't believe it.

The speed at which I had to work was unbelievable and I was pretty fit at that time. The line would stop for a ten minute tea break – you couldn't let the break drag on, otherwise there'd be a big pile up at the end of the line and you'd be in real trouble.

Eventually they moved me up the line and there was this older bloke who I felt sorry for – he was really struggling.

So I would do my own job, then dash up to him and do his job, then dash back to mine. I told him: "Pack this in – you're going to be ill." I saw him a few months later and he looked great. He said he'd left that job and was now working down the yard and he said philosophically: "I get next to nothing but I'm happy."

Vauxhall was one of the hardest jobs of my working life, no doubt about it. When I first went for it there were a few of us waiting to be interviewed. There was this fella opposite me, handsome, well dressed with a big sort of 'showbiz smile' on his face, and I thought: "God, I hope they don't put me with him."

Anyway when we'd got the jobs, they did put me with him, Richard Glynn his name was. He turned out to be a lovely fella.

A fab four in 1945: Sisters Doreen, Joyce, (a cute Charlie) and Sylvia

War baby: Nine months old and raring to go in 1942

Proud parents: Mum and dad, Aggie and Charles Alexander

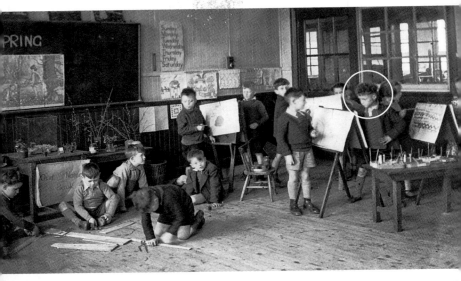

Portrait of the artist as a young man,
Charlie in his prime at primary school

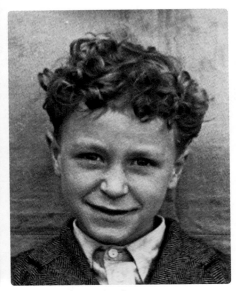

Ma and me: Aggie and son
on the doorstep at home

Boy wonder: Charlie at ten,
wondering what lies ahead

In my element: Back in 1955 aged 12, with winners' shield at Grange Secondary School

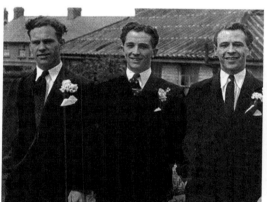

Relatively speaking: A great team – my brothers Arthur, Derek and Harry

Lighting up time for brother Arthur at a gig. And left Jack (with pint) and Ken Davies

Party time with sisters Dot,
Joyce, Sylvia and Doreen

Wetting the head with a difference:
About to be baptised at Wirral Christian Centre

No, not the Portland Primary School soccer
team, but me and my teaching colleagues

Me and Dave Carter
at the Pacific Pub

Dig the shirt: Me in 1972,
Engelbert Landsborough

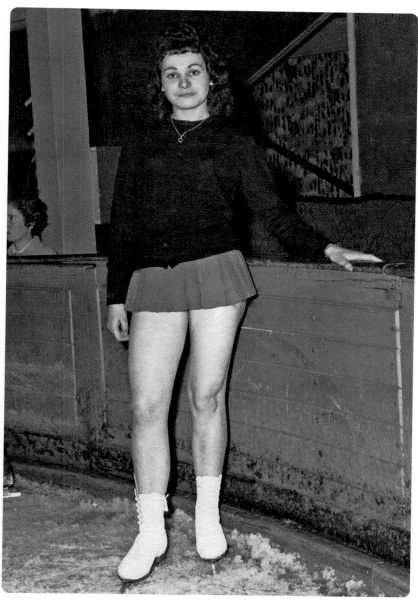

Skate expectations for me too:
Courting my wife to be Thelma

And in descending order, my
sons, Charlie, Allan and Jamie

He'd been in the famous Black and White Minstrels show and was a marvellous tenor. I think he'd won the Eisteddfod one year – the first time they had called somebody back to sing the song again.

Richard was picked up by a talent spotter and went to London to the Black and White Minstrels.

He said it was a bit of a revelation to him because a lot of the blokes in the minstrels were gay and he wasn't, and at first he was on the verge of having a fight every night. But he eventually talked to them like they were women and they talked to him like a woman to a man. I really got to know him and liked Richard.

Vauxhall was also very draining on me and when I did go out for the night with Thelma I'd very often end up falling asleep in a corner. But at the end bosses moved me from the gearbox line and that's what brought about another demise in my long career of demises. They took me across to this other block where there were a number of jobs in the 'finishing area.' There were a few of us there and I said: "I don't mind doing any sort of work, I'm not work-shy, but don't put me in the paint store."

I liked singing and I didn't want paint on my lungs. And the bloke in charge must have thought: "Right I'll show him."

Yeah, you've guessed it. Charlie and the Paint Factory. He dished all the jobs out and then said to me . . . "Paint shop."

And I said despairingly: "I asked you to please not put me in there because of my chest," and he just said: "Well that's it."

I said: "You can keep it."

But I'll let you in on a secret. I didn't leave quite as gracefully as that because I looked in the office and I thought it was a rather snide thing for that boss to do, and I put my coat on and in front of the others called out: "You are nothing but a snide and if I ever see you on the outside I'll punch you on the nose."

Then I stormed off home, a ten-mile walk from Ellesmere Port and that was the end of yet another job – gone, blowin' in the wind.

I often think about all the jobs I had. I got a job with Automatic Telephones, as it was called way back then, in Edge Lane in Liverpool, which was an awful long way from the North End of Birkenhead.

We didn't have any cars or anything like that to take me over there – it was public transport. And I was always hard up. I remember that I'd get there – I'd have my bus fare or boat fare, but in the dinner hour I'd be really hungry and I'd see a cake or something that I couldn't resist. Bang went my bus fare, so I'd have to walk to town.

The number of times I walked from Edge Lane to the Pier Head to get the boat was unbelievable. Anybody who knows Liverpool would know it's quite a walk. I think I used to get up at half six in the morning and I'd get home at half six at night, and that would be if I hadn't bought a cake. All of it for a very small amount of money at the time but I don't suppose it did me any harm.

I didn't last long there. Years later when I was navvying, I was working outside the Automatic Telephones place and by this time I had grown quite a bit. I was talking about it to a couple of the lads I worked with, whose names escape me now, and lo and behold one of these fellas walked past.

They used to take the mickey out of me – I was quite shy then, and they'd rib me and I'd explode, and offer them out for a fight, like.

They just laughed at me which made it worse, you know. One of these lads was passing, they were nice lads really, and I went up and tapped him on the shoulder and said: "Hello mate, you don't remember me do you?"

And he said "No."

And he looked a little bit worried to be honest, so I said: "I'm Charlie, I used to be an apprentice here years ago.

"And you and the other fella used to take the mickey out of me something awful, we used to play football in the dinner hour and you were always taking the mickey out of me."

He said: "Oh I didn't mean nothing." I think he thought I was going to belt him or something, so I said: "I know you didn't, mate. I'm not bothered about that.

"It's funny I was just talking about you and you walk past. How are you?" And I think he looked at me with a little bit of pity in his eyes.

He must have thought, look at the state of him with a pair of wellies on digging down a hole, and I thought, well, I felt a little bit sorry for him because at least I'd been around a bit.

I'd been in the army and a few places and everything, and I'd done a few different things. And I thought, Frank, that was his name, he's been coming in and out of here all those years in between. So I don't know who felt more sorry for who.

# 5. Twenty-Two Not Out

AS John Lennon once sang in the beautiful ballad *In My Life*, there are some places and people we will never forget.

I will always have very fond memories of playing in the North Star pub and the great Vera Elliott coming in, or sending someone over to ask if we'd play every week for a fiver in her pub The Pacific, and I thought we'd cracked it, you know?

It was a fantastic pub in those days and she was a great boss and that's half the battle when you are playing regularly – a good supportive mine host. Vera would book different bands and characters turning up all through the night and it was a fantastic atmosphere. I was there for 22 years playing in that place. That's some residency. I finished up just doing the Sunday dinner hour and the Sunday night in the end.

Sunday afternoons were probably my favourite time of all, because you'd go in on a nice day, and the lounge would be absolutely choc-a-bloc, with the sun streaming in through the windows. Even looking at the pints was a bit of a mystical experience (drinking them was just as good) and all the lights would be shining on them.

There was a lot of good-natured humour in there. The only trouble was, poor Thelma. I just couldn't stop singing and performing at that time, and I'd finish my stint, they'd close the pub then I'd start singing again.

I'd come home late, have my tea and then go back for the evening. And when the night finished and they closed the doors, I'd stay on singing. That's all I was doing – I was just enthralled by the music. And the lads liked a little bit of a musical backdrop to their sessions.

No harm was done, but it certainly wasn't fair on Thelma.

One of the pubs we played in was the Long Bar in Liverpool on the Dock Road, run by Alma and her husband, Robert.

They were lovely people. I remember the pub because one of the first songs that I wrote was called *Still Around* and I tell the story to this day of performing that song on this night. You know I never announced it because I thought if people laughed at it they'd never know it was mine. Cowardly I suppose, really. But I just sang it and got a polite round of applause but later on it got more attention. It only takes one person to say how much they liked it.

The Long Bar was a really smashing place. I remember me and Kenny were booked by this bloke who'd just opened a new club in New Brighton, and he wanted to try and build it up.

We had a little reputation locally and so we turned up. It was only just open and there was hardly anybody in there and we were stood at the bar having a glass before we set our stuff up. There was only an American and his girlfriend in the other room – she was English – and this fella came to the bar and got talking to us. He was a right character and called himself Jason Demetrius. I think probably his name was Billy Smith or something like that, but I liked him. I love eccentrics and characters, and he asked what sort of stuff did we play? So I said we did all sorts and that Kenny did instrumentals, like Zorba The Greek, the soundtrack from a famous film.

"Oh I love that stuff," he says, "That's fantastic."

So he says to the barman: "Hey Barkeeper, how much is half a glass of bitter?" It wasn't a lot, but he counted out the little bit of change in his hand and shrugged and then said: "I shall be back in two shakes of a lamb's tail."

He disappeared and came back with just enough to buy this glass. Then he says: "I've done a lot of choreography myself you know."

Well I thought this fella's either a genius or a complete madman, in the nicest sense. I was right the second time. I usually am because I've met that many people and I cherish the memories of those I've come across.

We'd just kicked off the set, and there was just the American and his girlfriend, and this fella and us in the room.

Kenny started playing Zorba The Greek and this Jason bloke leapt into the air and threw himself all around the room falling over everything, but with a straight face and obviously totally wrapped up in what he was doing. To the great surprise of this American and his girl, he was hurling himself about the room in a most ungainly manner, which I thought was absolutely marvellous. So I think I bought him a couple of drinks because I loved his company.

Later on a crowd started coming in and he said: "I wonder if I could get up and sing?"

I said of course, yes, he could. So we called him up and he said to the watching crowd: "I've met this lovely girl and I've written this song myself about her. She's a beautiful girl and this is my song."

I forget the girl's name but let's say it was Denise. He got ready and said to us: "Key of C, please" (I don't know what key he was singing in, and neither did he).

Then he went on like this (you will have to imagine the scenario).

"I was walking through the park and I saw this girl and she looked very nice and I said you look very nice . . ." and it went on like this for about ten minutes, all spoken. And that was it – his own composition.

Everybody was rolling around laughing, but he was completely oblivious to this. Halfway through, he got fed up and broke into the traditional song *Hang Down Your Head Tom Dooley* in a falsetto voice, and people were tossing pennies onto the stage.

I loved Jason – I don't know what happened to him but he certainly lit up that night.

I loved working with Kenny on and off stage. Kenny and I worked for the Gas Board, and for a while we worked in the same gang, until unfortunately he was put in a different one. I got word one day that he'd had an accident and been involved in an explosion of some kind and had got burnt. I had to go round to the house to see if he was alright.

Now Kenny was only a little fellow and he had a moustache, and when I arrived he was sat there and it was like something off a cartoon – his tache was all singed, his eyebrows were singed, his hair was singed and his nose was red, and I could only just hold myself back from laughing.

He was ok, apart from a little bit of singeing, but he just looked so sorry for himself with his singed tache. He'll never forgive me when he reads this. Kenny and I split up the duo to do different things after being together for many years, and I joined forces with a lovely lad who's not long passed away – Davy Carter. He was very handsome and a fine guitar player. We struck it up together and played the Pacific and a number of other pubs.

Now Davy wasn't particularly fond of regular work, like many of us, and this particular day we were in the Pacific when this fella came over and said to Davy: "Are you working?" and he replied, "No, but I'm looking around for something."

Little Billy Suckley was behind him – Billy Brillo we called him because of his close cropped hair cut – and said: "If you're after a job I'll get you a form for the yard," (Cammell Laird).

Dave's face got longer by the minute. Sure enough, that night Billy turns up with the form and gives it to Dave who says: "Oh thanks, I'll fill it in, in the morning."

"No you won't," says Billy, "You can fill it in now and I'll take it in with me."

Dave's face was a joy to behold. And he filled it in and got the job, which was the last thing in the world he wanted actually. I thought that was great. He did actually work down the yard for a short while.

I remember Davy's dad, Alan, who was a great character. He always smoked a pipe and – this was the first time I saw this – his teeth had worn away where his pipe fitted perfectly.

He used to tell me I should learn to sing like Foster and Allen, but I could only play like ME. One day his lads got hold of his pipe and put a bit of cannabis in it. And he sat in his armchair and he grew the widest smile on by the minutes as he smoked it. He never knew what was in it, but he said it was the best smoke he'd ever had.

In those days lots of people were smoking it but I never touched the stuff. My only drug was alcohol, I loved a pint of Guinness, you know. I remember sitting there one day and I think I had five pints of Guinness – the lads were piling them up, even though you had one, someone else would get you one and I ended up with five pints.

Ned Starkey looked up and said: "Look at that – it looks like the Brazilian forward line."

There was a time when I packed up completely for about three years and only drank water. I'd be playing in these rough pubs, on my own at the time, and I'd go to the bar and ask for a glass of water and you'd see these fellas looking at me like there was something wrong with me but I did it, and it did me a lot of good.

I'd disappear as soon as the gig was over and Thelma was delighted because I was coming home early and I was coming home sober. It was wonderful – I should have kept it up really.

# 6. Enter Charlie the Feet

THOSE early gigs shaped me and I met some lovely characters along the way.

In those days I rarely played anything of my own. It was all cover versions. I did everything – anything – that I thought I could play reasonably well including old rock and roll, old blues standards, Irish songs, folk, ballads, bits of Bing Crosby and stuff like that. Anything at all that I liked I decided I would do.

I thoroughly enjoyed it and loved finding songs that nobody else had ever covered like B sides and things like that, and they'd become quite popular in the pub, thankfully, because I liked them so much myself. What the lads liked most, was when it was late, when they'd say "Give us the window cleaner, Charl," and *The Window Cleaner* – well it went on for ages and ages.

My brothers Arthur, Derek and Jack used to sing little medleys, like *When I'm Cleaning Windows* and then an old Country song, and they'd just mix it up. I learned from what they had done and I just kept adding to it. One day in the pub I thought I'll do that, and did my own medley, and every time I thought of something I just went on into the next song and it really did go on for a long time – I'm not talking about five or ten minutes, or even fifteen minutes, it went on for ages.

I'd also do bits of other George Formby hits, then I'd do chunks of country music – there was all sorts thrown into this and they loved it because, apart from anything else, Vera would be calling Last Orders and she'd be shouting, "Charlie, have you seen the time?" and the lads would be saying: "Keep going," so they'd all get extra time and Vera would be smiling because although it was late the house was full and everybody was seriously having a good time.

There were a couple of dock lads working together – one was from Birkenhead and the other was from across the water.

They were arguing about bands. The Wirral fella obviously liked what we were doing in the duet, and he said to the Liverpudlian: "You want to see this duo we've got on our side (of the river)," and the Liverpool lad said: "You think they're good, you want to see this pair that I go to see on a Saturday."

At that particular time, if we got a booking and were asked what we called ourselves, we'd just tell them to give us whatever name they liked. And so, of course, we had a variety of names including some very odd ones. In one place we were called The Ring Boys, I don't know what that was supposed to denote! But we'd get a bit of amusement out of turning up and seeing who we were that night.

When we played in the Pacific we were just Charlie and Kenny, but when we played The Goat in Liverpool, they'd booked us as 'The Atlantics.' I think they'd heard about the pub we played in Birkenhead and got the wrong ocean.

So, anyway, these two lads are arguing about which is the best duo and they decided to have a bet on it, and go one night to the Pacific and the next night to The Goat. Of course when they got to the Pacific they realised they'd been talking about the same duo, which was very gratifying for us. Neither of them, however, won the bet.

Coming through the Mersey Tunnel was always a nightmare – I didn't have very reliable cars, we'd driven out to this gig in Liverpool and at that time I hadn't passed my test. There was me, Kenny, and this big lad called Tommy and all the gear in the back in an old heap and as we got near the tunnel the exhaust dropped off.

I tried to tie it up with a guitar string, believe it or not (oh you do!) so it was a really botched up job. As we came out of the tunnel this policeman pulled us up, and I had L-plates on (the car not me).

The copper said: "You've just lost your exhaust system in the tunnel. Pull over there." I thought we were really in trouble and I said: "Look, I don't really want it can't I just go home?"

He said: "No, you certainly can't go home – you stay there," but I got away with it, well with a caution, and being told to "watch my step" and make sure my vehicle was roadworthy in future. Exhausting, indeed.

I always hated that run through the tunnel because my cars were so unreliable. One night I was coming through on my own, and I'd just made it through the toll on my side of the river, when the car conked out. And this lad in an equally old heap pulled up behind me, jumped out and said: "What's the matter pal?" So I told him the car was clapped out and he said, "Jump in and I'll push you home." And he did, he bumped me home to the North end of Birkenhead.

Now that sounds ridiculous, and it was but his car was an old banger anyway and it was very generous of him. Things were a lot more relaxed on the roads then.

I always loved gigging even if getting to the venue was a hassle. You always met great people. I was playing in a pub one Sunday lunchtime and this very well dressed, David Niven type man came in and sat down, and every time I looked up he seemed absolutely delighted with what Kenny and I were playing which was lovely.

At the end he came over and said how much he'd enjoyed it and we got talking and I got to know him really well. He was called Les Jenkins. Les once asked me whose song it was I was singing. It was a Tom Paxton number and when I told him he then went out and bought about four Paxton albums.

But the following week he came in with all of them and gave them to me and said he didn't like him singing the songs – he preferred me – which was nice because I got all these free Paxton albums.

I got to know Les really well and we'd go to the golf courses together. He was a watch-maker in Lewis's department store at that time. He had a good job, a lovely house and a good car, whereas we didn't have much – we were a bit of a motley crew, but we'd still go to the golf.

Golf was a good relaxation. I'd strike off but I couldn't wait to get away because I wasn't much good, and neither was Cliffy who was with us. Les would be swinging away there, full of confidence not caring about these proper golfers who were behind him, all studying his stance and his swing and everything. He'd take a few swings, and you could see them nodding and looking approvingly, then he'd take this almighty swing and miss completely and they'd step back in amazement and think perhaps it was another practice swing.

It never was.

Then he took another swing, and hit the top of the ball, and it dropped off like a fried egg, so he picked it up and put it back again.

By this time his reputation had dwindled somewhat among the onlookers, and when he did hit it, it scurried along the ground like a grass snake for about forty yards. Nonchalantly he said: "That'll do me," pulled up his trolley and swung off along the course. And there's me and the other fellas there in total embarrassment.

He never really cared about his golf skills but he was very good-hearted. He once went into the golf house to get the trolleys for us and came out with a brand new one which he gave to me. He'd just bought it for me.

It was very sad much later – he lost his job and everything seemed to go wrong for him. It was really tragic to see because I thought the world of him. I remember him phoning me asking to give him a hand once. He'd got two punctures – only Les could get TWO punctures, but we went and sorted it out.

He eventually bought a little green grocer's in Cleveland Street Birkenhead. He was doing watches in the upstairs while his wife ran the green grocery downstairs. He called it The Clockwork Orange which I thought was a very appropriate name. A great character.

Sadly a few years later Les got cancer. He wasn't in the best of health, and then one day when he was out in his car with his wife, a stolen vehicle driven by a couple of lads crashed into him and he was killed. It was horrible, but perhaps it saved him a lot of suffering because he wasn't well at all.

I met some very funny characters when I started playing the country music clubs.

Some people really take it seriously and I remember playing in Bury – a really pleasant night with nice people – in a place called The Silverado country music club. Great name.

The following week I was playing in a little pub in Rochdale upstairs, just on my own this time with a guitar and a set of bass pedals – more of that later – although Thelma was with me, and I went up to the bar to get us a couple of drinks.

There was this fella there, who was dressed very smartly, albeit as a sheriff, complete with badge and a big hat – lovely bloke and he was telling me how much he enjoyed my music.

"Much better than that other Welsh lot," he said, referring to a duo who I thought were very good actually, but he dismissed them saying: "Whoever heard of a Welsh cowboy?"

And there was he, from Rochdale, dressed as a sheriff. And he was deadly serious, so I just said: "Maybe you're right," and I went and sat down. But I thought that was lovely.

I was playing in another country music club in Shrewsbury and, again, I was getting a pre-show drink at the bar and there was this bloke there who got talking to me about the music. He spoke in a sort of pseudo-American accent, and he told me that he came to that club every week but then added: "I'm a bit sad because I should have been married on Saturday, but I guess I'm just a drifter."

This is Shrewsbury I thought. He then said: "Do me a favour, partner, play a song for me?"

So I said: "Yeah, sure, who should I say it's for?"

He said: "Just dedicate it to Black Bart."

Black Bart . . . I love all that eccentricity out there.

Back in Rochdale I remember setting things up, getting the pedals ready and everything else and there was a band there.

It was only a small place but I thought, that's good there's a group on as well. There was this fella reading the paper, watching these lads and he goes over to them and asks who they were and they said they were called Wagon Wheel and he said: "You're not on here – Charlie the Feet's playing here tonight."

He called me Charlie the Feet because of my bass pedals. It sounds like a Mafia hit man doesn't it? But it turned out they'd got the wrong place and it was just going to be me.

I remember when I decided to go my own way, after playing in a duo with other people for years, I was a bit apprehensive to say the least. I'd always wanted a set of bass pedals to play with my feet – that always fascinated me, and I thought it would be great if I could do that.

I was telling Kenny this and he told me I could buy them and he showed me a set in a magazine that was for sale. Well I bought them. Thelma wasn't convinced, she said: "You'll look ridiculous, you don't even know if you can play them, you can't afford them, and you'll look absolutely stupid."

Well I was playing them the following week – friends of ours Barbara and Paul Brassey had a place in Ullapool, a lovely motel, and they said they'd give us a free holiday if I'd come and play in the bar. So I took these pedals up and played and I never stopped playing them for a long, long time after that.

That, dear friends, is how I became Charlie the Feet.

I couldn't play them with my shoes on – I had to play them in my socks. People recognised my feet more than my face. It liberated me really.

That pub in Rochdale was run by Jack and his wife with their daughter, and they'd get up between sets and do a little session on their own.

Jack was always forgetting things. He was wonderful at doing monologues, but they'd be standing there talking amongst themselves while he remembered what they should do next.

He'd pick a song, and then he'd be asking the people in the front row how it went. Anyway I turned up this night and set up and he was compering that night. So Jack gets up to introduce me and says, "Ladies and gentlemen, it's marvellous that you're all here and I'd like you to give a big welcome to our old friend er, Charlie, erm, Farnborough, ooh no, that's a bloke at work, no it's erm our friend Charlie."

And he shot off. I loved him and his forgetfulness.

The first big gig that I did – well to me it was huge – was when I was working for a fella called Neil Coppendale who ran the Worthing Country Music Festival in the lovely Worthing Pavilion.

They asked me could I come down and do a little slot. Well I'd never played anywhere like that and I was terrified. But I got on the train with Thelma and we went down all the way to Worthing.

I just had a guitar – they brought me on and I did a couple of songs with a band they had. I was a bag of nerves. But it went down really well and that was the first big gig that I'd ever done, you know.

We went back on the train – I don't think I got anything for it.

But it was my initiation.

# 7. In the Army Now

I JOINED the army on March 20, 1961 and I was in there for four years and 48 days.

I remember how I came to join, because I'd seen my brothers return from the merchant navy all tanned with lovely clothes on – all fit and healthy and everything with a few bob in their pocket. I always wanted to be like them.

I tried to join the merchant navy by going to one of the schools, but I was either too young for some of them or too old for others so I couldn't get in. I thought I'd join the Royal Navy and the office was closed, but around the corner was the Army office, so I joined the Army. I just desperately wanted to get away from Birkenhead.

I went home that day and my dad, because he was getting on to me at the time, said: "Have you got a job yet?" and I said: "Yeah, I've got a job and it's for nine years." He said: "Nine years? What's that?" I said: "I've joined the army. " Well, my sisters were upset, but off I tootled and I joined the Royal Artillery.

When I joined up I was sent to do my training in Oswestry. I remember walking through the gates – I had my DA (Ducks Arse) hair style at that time – I was carrying my guitar and I walked through and stopped and spoke to two regimental policemen, and asked them: "Where's 24 Irish battery mate?"

And they said: "Just down there," with a big smile on their faces, because they knew what was coming.

Needless to say my DA didn't last long. In fact it was only a day or so later that they took us all down to the barbers.

Now I haven't got the sort of head that suits short hair at all, and I went in and said to the barber: "Listen, I know you've got to cut my hair but just take a bit off and I'll sort you out."

He said: "Oh, alright mate," and the next thing I felt the shears on the top of my head. It didn't work at all, so I came out to the same howls of ridicule as everybody else.

The training was really hard – I was room captain and I think I won the cross country and everything.

We had a good outfit really, but it was hard going and we had the bullying and all that. I remember this lad in our room and all the other lads called him Flossy and I told them to leave him alone. I thought it was just because he spoke a bit nicer than everybody else, and that wasn't very fair. I was defending him and they sent us on a 15-mile march through Wales, and we were absolutely shattered when we got to the camp.

Some of the lads were going up the road for a pint, but I didn't have any money so I said I wouldn't go. They'd paired me with this Flossy lad this night and I got into my sleeping bag to go off asleep while he went with the rest of the lads to the pub.

The next thing I remember is this hand fondling my nether regions. I woke up furious but still shattered. And I yelled at him that I'd batter him in the morning.

In the morning he was nowhere to be seen and was sat up on a hill well away from me. I never mentioned it to any of the others because they'd have given him a really hard time. But he stayed well away from me forever after that. It was a lesson in guessing characters and I was wrong there – Flossy was a bit of a Flossy.

After training, they sent me down to Salisbury Plain, to Lark Hill. It was just right by Stonehenge – you could just about see the stone circle from our camp. That wasn't bad but it was a bit of an eye opener because I'd thought it was going to be all action and running around with guns in your hands and all that sort of stuff.

The first morning they were sending us all off everywhere, and they said to two of us: "You and you are off to the Sergeant's Mess." And I thought I wonder what's this all about. I soon found out – I was in the Sergeant's Mess for two weeks washing pots and pans.

I thought I've joined the army to be a housewife.

Anyway. I kicked up about that and the next day I was out on parade again and I thought I've got out of that. And he said: "Right, Landsborough – the coke heap."

They sent me around the back where there were these mounds of coke and he said: "Right. Level that off." So I had to spend the day levelling these mounds. It was just a pointless exercise to keep me in my place. I came back black as the Ace of Spades.

I was quickly getting the idea that it wasn't all action. In fact I remember one of the lads, younger than me – we called him Devil Doran – and he was always on parade. He came up to me and asked: "When do we get to throw the grenades and all that?" We told him 'no', you get to wash pots and pans and level coke heaps. The name Devil Doran stuck with him all the time he was in our camp.

When I was down in Salisbury, because I'd had a bit of an education, they put me down to train as a meteorologist. I later discovered how dangerous that could have been, because they told me that if war had ever broken out meteorologists or surveyors were only given about two days survival expectancy. I didn't stay a Met Man very long, and I can't remember a thing about the weather. But I enjoyed that little bit of learning stimulus, it wasn't bad at all.

After Salisbury they moved me to Rhyl, North Wales, and I was so naive in those days when I went there – I think I had my 21st birthday while I was there.

I remember walking into this big camp and asking where the battery was that I was in and the fella said: "Just up there, Scouse."

And I thought how did he know that I was a Scouser. I must have thought I spoke really well.

There was a character there called Bob Close, who I really didn't like when I first met him, I nearly fought him, but I got to know him and like him – he was a real character. Me and him had quite a bit of fun. They put him in a room with a load of old sweats, as we called them – I don't think they were very old but they were much older than us but they'd been in the army a long time, and they were looking very cynically at us.

Bob would stroll into the room, full of life, and they'd all be lying in their pits, and he'd shout: "Ok you lot get some in" meaning put some time in and you should have seen the looks on their faces, you know, they hated him. But I liked him and we had great fun.

It's amazing the daft things you do – I'm afraid of heights but when I was in Rhyl I thought I'd join the paratroopers and that would cure me. I thought, when I see someone else doing it I'll want to do it. But thankfully now, the Sergeant told me I had no chance unless I smartened myself up. I was a bit of rebel without a cause then. Needless to say I never got to go there and now I think, thank God I didn't. I'd have probably killed myself.

With typical army logic, when I was out in Rhyl they asked me where I would like to be posted and I asked to go to Hong Kong.

I thought that's great, it's the other end of the earth it'll be marvellous there. So they sent me to Germany.

But as it happened I'm glad they did because I really enjoyed my stint there. I remember flying over there and it was winter when we flew – it was freezing. I never looked much cop in the uniform anyway, but those stiff collars really rubbed my neck raw and you couldn't take them off because you were in the army weren't you?

But we had some nice little fires in the rooms and we'd take some bread from the cookhouse and we'd sit in the evening cooking our toast.

And then I started to teach myself German and because of that I had a great time. I'd learn a few things and then go and try them out – foreigners like it if you make an attempt to learn their language.

I saw this phrase which meant 'It's both cheap and good.' So I thought, well, I can use that, it's a good phrase. I was with this girl and I meant to say: "You're young and pretty," and instead I said: "You're both cheap and good." I got a smack around the ear – and I didn't have enough German to explain how I'd made the mistake.

Needless to say that little relationship didn't last.

I had some fun with the language. I was in an out-of-bounds pub – don't know why it was out-of-bounds because it was similar to a number of other pubs that were ok – but there were a number of us in there and I was in my civvies. I had some German clothes at the time, and I was sat on my own talking to these Germans.

The MPs came in throwing all the squaddies out and I just sat where I was. This corporal came over and tapped me and said: "Outside."

I just said back to him in German: "You're joking aren't you? I'm having a drink with my friends now beat it."

He went a bit red in the face and all the Germans were laughing. He went over to the Sergeant and said: "See him over there? I'm sure he's a squaddie. He looked too anaemic to be a German."

But they had to leave me there because they couldn't risk it and when they left all the Germans gave me a round of applause. I didn't stay long after that but it was nice to have a little bit of fun at officialdom's expense.

I used to phone the guardroom when I knew some of the lads would be on and say in German: "Can I have a taxi to the corner of Station Road?" and the lads would say: "What?"

They'd try to talk back to me and pass the phone to each other and I remember one of them even saying: "Waitin ze ein minute." Now isn't that a classic piece of German?

And then after a couple of minutes the penny would drop and they'd say, "It's that bloody Scouse having us on again." They'd mutter a profanity or two, then I'd hang up. But they never collared me for it, it was just a little bit of fun.

There was a little regimental military policeman looking after our camp who didn't like big fellas, and he hated me in particular.

I don't know what I'd done to him. Orders came on the notice board that read: "It has come to our attention that some of the ranks have been taking bread and provisions from the cookhouse to take back to their quarters and this has got to stop immediately. Anybody found doing so will be severely dealt with."

Anyway, the cookhouse was right opposite the guard room, and I knew he'd be watching, so I came out of the cookhouse with all of the lads surrounding me, looking very suspicious with my hand up my jumper, and I knew he'd think he'd got me.

I could see his head bobbing up and down, and the glee on his face, and he came charging out of the guard room thinking, "I've got him."

"Landsborough step out here," he said. "Get out of the way you lot."

"This is victimisation," I said, and all the lads were backing me up, but he carried on, "Lift the jumper up, let's see what you've got under there," with a big smile on his face.

I complained a bit more but he repeated it again, so I lifted up the jumper and there behind it was a perfect V sign. His face went bright red, and all the lads doubled up with laughter. If he hated me before, he did more after that, but it was worth it.

Bob Close turned up at our camp. He was a bit of a lad back home and the police just didn't like him. I don't think he'd done anything disastrously wrong. They pulled him up once because he didn't have a rear illuminator bulb. When they'd asked him if he had anything to say for himself he said: "Yes tell Laura I love her."

I think he got a 20 pound fine. He was going home on leave, and he had this car – he was banned from driving at the time – and he was going home in it. I warned him against it because I knew the police would have him, but he said he knew all the back roads and he'd be fine.

I didn't see him again for about two years. He lived in Buckinghamshire, and when he went home this time he was going down all the back lanes but this was the night of the Great Train Robbery, and the whole of the countryside was awash with police. So they caught him. But what a character.

It was while I was in this camp in Germany that one of the lads said that the other regiment up the road were looking for a singer.

"Why don't you have a go?" he said. So I went over and had a little audition with these other squaddies and they gave me the job. Well that was a marvellous doorway to the local social life for me.

We used to play in the local pubs – the band was called The Rock Avons and I was the singer. Obviously all the girls liked us so that was an introduction to young ladies which was smashing.

I also remember this lad from Leicestershire who didn't know how to look after himself with the girls. He'd say: "Can you take us down and introduce us to the girls?"

And I'd say: "Smarten yourself up. Look at you, clean your teeth." I was acting like his dad: "and look at your shirt, wash it and press it." In the end he looked very smart. But he had to pay me to take him into town – he had to do my washing and ironing to pay me back. He did it because he was that desperate to meet the girls. In fact he's still living in Germany to this day – he married one of the girls that he met through me and the music.

And he finished up being quite a smart lad – I think he became a telephone engineer in Germany.

So that turned out quite well for him.

# 8. Two-Fingered Salute

IN some respects I was a bit of a nuisance in the army – I didn't do anything dreadfully wrong I was just slightly anti-authority.

They put me in the stores, which was a nice soft job. They put another lad with me and then they sent me this really eccentric one called Paul – incredibly bright – I think he could speak three languages fluently, but he was away with the mixer in other things.

Everybody loved him, he was a lovely little fella. I said to him on his first day: "You'll be alright here Paul, in the morning – we take turns in getting up – I'll get up and open the Store – you can have a bit of a lie in. If there's anything needed I'll come and get you. But you have a lie in and get up and washed about half nine and tootle down to the Store."

By our room, there was this passageway all the way down to the store with offices, with the officers themselves in them. About half nine in the morning there's Paul looking like a dishevelled Stan Laurel, with a towel and soap in his hand strolling down past all the officers, looking like a bag of rubbish, and calling "Good Morning" to them all. You could see them staring at him so I pulled him to one side and explained that he should look like he's been up for hours when he goes past the officers. But he was a good lad.

This same Paul kept messing up every job he'd been given, for all his intelligence. I was just about the last one – he'd even been given a job at the piggery and he'd let all the pigs out.

But he was an absolute gem. Old Jim, God bless him, the Sergeant Major in charge of the Store, came down when we had a consignment and he was peering over his spectacles and organised us into a line with another lad to put everything on the shelves.

Paul was throwing everything everywhere. Jim would try to explain again what he wanted Paul to do and he couldn't get over how Paul just couldn't get it.

He'd be in his own world, and you'd see him and say, "Hello" to him and there'd be nothing, until a minute after you'd passed him you'd hear this distant voice saying: "Hello Charl." He was brilliant and was loved by even the hard cases.

Big Ginger from Liverpool and his hard case cronies put it around that Paul was a Martial Arts expert, and that he'd battered Big Ginger – the more he denied it the more he was believed.

I remember him playing cards, and winning because he was clever, and he ended up deliberately losing, because he realised they were getting a bit fed up with losing. So he lost it all back to them – he didn't like the ill feeling that winning was creating.

This job could get a bit boring, and we used to think up daft things to break the boredom. This Scotch fella came in to get a pair of socks, or something, and I said: "Have you had your coat scuttle inspected? There's a big inspection and one of the big noises is coming to the camp and they're checking everything. And it's our job to inspect all the coal scuttles in the camp."

He didn't believe me but I carried on: "Please yourself, but we have the facilities here for rectifying if there's anything wrong with it." He said: "That's rubbish."

"Ok it's no skin off my nose," I said. "Forget it, but if you're in trouble don't come to me."

Anyway he shot off and next thing you could hear this clanging and he showed up with this coal scuttle. We put it on a desk and we're inspecting it from all angles and I wrote a note in German for the little German cobbler who had his office further down: "Would you please stud this coat scuttle?"

We sent Jock off to him with the scuttle and the note and we were looking out of the door after him. The little cobbler came out then scratching his head and Jock realised we'd been taking the mickey.

And he went clanging off. But whenever we'd see him in the canteen after that we asked: "How's your coal scuttle?"

So that was good fun.

In the same stores, little Taffy came in looking for a new boiler suit, saying: "If I don't have one I'll get put on a charge."

I told him we hadn't got one, but he said again: "I've got to have one." So I said: "Well we have got one but it's the only one and it's no good to you because it's outsize."

We had lots really but we just wanted to have a laugh. So he says: "I've got to have it. Give us it." He looked like the famous Michelin Man in it, there were folds everywhere and we watched him shooting out in it. He didn't get put on a charge, and we did change it for him but we had a good laugh out of that, anyway.

Now we were only a couple of miles from the East German border, and apparently if anything had happened they didn't expect us to last more than a day or two. They had these series of exercises called Quick Train, and they could come at any time – usually when you'd been out and had a few beers, you know? I remember this night suddenly hearing this Quick Train and having to get up, pull all my gear on and get on parade in the square.

Now me being in the Store, I had a handcart which I was supposed to put all the clothes on but I just piled up with socks. I remember thinking, there's these lads on parade ready to run, and there's me in with a hand cart. But that was the army. If the Russians had attacked I wouldn't have got far would I?

It was the time of the Cuban missile crisis and I was terrified, I was convinced that this was it. But rather than stay fretting in the camp I thought I'd go into town and have a few pints. I might as well go and enjoy myself – I'll be dead in the morning.

I was walking back, and this was a NATO camp with lots of different camps with different nationalities, and everywhere you went was a hive of activity.

People were loading stuff into tanks by searchlight – Germans were working on the tanks, the Danes were loading tanks, and the Yanks and the Canadians, they were all working away. I thought, "Oh God this is serious and it is really all going to kick off."

I got back to our camp and there was not a sign of life anywhere. And what were our lads doing?

They were polishing the doorknobs and buffing the floors in readiness for an inspection in the morning. I said: "Well isn't that marvellous? If the Russians had attacked, they'd have taken us in an instant. And they'd have thought well, they weren't very good squaddies, these British, but they didn't half keep the place nice and clean." But thankfully nothing happened, and I was so grateful.

We got officers when we were in this particular camp who were as young, some younger, than us. Obviously you are supposed to salute officers. I used to have great fun – you could see them waiting agitatedly stiffening their arm to salute, once you had saluted them first. I could see this young officer coming towards us, and I was looking at him from the corner of my eye, and I waited till he got close and then I shot my arm up and he shot his arm up in salute, but I scratched my head.

He went bright red and the lads were laughing and he said: "Landsborough, you're supposed to salute," so I said, "Oh I'm sorry sir, I didn't see you." And it came on orders the following day: It has come to our attention that certain officers have not been receiving their due salutation, or whatever it is. In future all officers shall be saluted whether seen or not. So we were all walking around for a few days after that just saluting thin air.

I remember some lovely Irish character, who wasn't the brightest spark in the world, God bless him, and they were going to send a helicopter to the camp for helicopter training, and Paddy was worried about this. He asked me if I'd done it before. So I said: "Yes, Paddy, there's nothing to it."

I hadn't. And so he asked: "What do they do?" Our building was really high.

I said: "See that roof on our building? Well the helicopter hovers about twenty feet over that and they drop a rope down and you just swarm down the rope over and then you drop off. And that's it. It's dead easy."

Horror spread over his face. "Now how high is that?" he says, "D'you know?"

"Don't worry Paddy there's only two people died in the last seven years. It's a doddle."

Paddy went missing the following day. And all it was – the helicopter landed and you ran and got in it and got off again. There was no height involved in it at all. But the officers were very kindly toward him and he never got into trouble for that, which I was thankful for.

Before they put me in the Store, they'd tried to make me a batman. I thought, I'm not going to be a housewife to some officer. I really resented that, you know. They told me to go to this officer's house to work there. So I went, and the lady of the house came to the door and I said I'd come for the officer's shoes. She brought out these two pairs of shoes, and I just brought them back to the camp.

And I just stayed in the camp and I think all I did for the next three days was polish these two pair of shoes. Because the camp thought I was at the officer's house and the officer thought I was in the camp. That was my only taste of being a bat man.

I didn't want to be a bat man because the wives and the children would treat you like a little slave.

Some people loved it but I could never have done it.

There used to be a character back in Birkenhead called Terry Connell who talked gibberish – a bit Stanley Unwinish – so inspired by this I thought I'd have some fun. I was with little Taffy, cleaning up in the stores and I was just about to go off, and said that I had a message from the Regimental Sergeant Major (RSM) who was a nasty piece of work.

Taffy looked worried and said: "What is it?"

So I said "chewin a guna tain him tomorrafternoon half past three so be there."

He said: "You what? Could you repeat that please?"

So I repeated it and he said: "Oh, come on Scouse, say it slowly."

"Are you taking the mickey out of me now?" I said. "I'll tell you again but I'm going out on a date so I'm going then. And if you're not there it's your fault."

I repeated it for him again and again, and he followed me about as I went to get washed and he kept asking me to repeat and I pretended to get fed up. In the end I shot off and nothing happened to him of course because the RSM hadn't said anything. But after that I used to see him and say: "Chewin a guna tain him?"

And he'd say: "Go 'way Scouse." So that was a little bit of fun.

I'd use the same technique with Jim. I'd go in and see him, pretending to be angry, and the lads used to watch through a hole in the wall. The same routine happened, but he was very patient and he used to try and understand it because he wanted to keep me in the stores.

He was great – he knew that we had a good job in the Store, and there'd be days when we were doing nothing, but he always used to give us a little warning that he was coming – he'd hum to himself like a trumpet as he walked along the passage so we'd know to look busy. But this particular day, we couldn't resist it. He came in and said he wanted to inspect the blouses.

I said: "Right Sir!" and I gave a little trumpet and then turned to the other lad and said: "You check the blouses, and I'll check the trousers."

I trumpeted, and the other lad trumpeted, and after a couple of minutes of us all humming like trumpets, the penny dropped. Poor Jim never did anything, but I don't think we got any more trumpet warnings after that.

There was a lovely old dear who used to be the cleaner there, and I learned to sing *Silent Night* in German to her. She loved it. We used to sing it together in the passageway of a night. I've done a version of *O Christmas Tree* in German as well – I think they sound lovely in their original language.

It was freezing when we first arrived in Germany, and when I heard they were looking for someone to work in the sergeants' mess, I thought, that'll be good it'll be warm in there. So me and Bob put our hands up. Well I should have learned my lesson from the first camp I'd ever been in. We were just housewives washing up, making beds. All the sergeants were living in – there were no married quarters set up then.

It came to a head when I lost my temper and said something acerbic to a Sergeant Major. He lost his temper back at me. But it was worth it because that was the last day I did in the mess. I went back with the lads after that.

I went in the NAAFI one day, with the lads, and I ordered a cup of coffee and a cheese sandwich. I took a bite out of it and then started talking, and when I looked at the sandwich again I saw this bit of black. And it was a cockroach – or half a cockroach – I'd eaten the other half. I went back to the lady behind the counter and showed her and she just said: "Oh I'll get you another one."

It was a pointless argument really. We laughed about it – it wouldn't have been so bad if I'd seen a whole one. But half a one doesn't leave you with a very pleasant feeling.

Because I was in a band, I used to be out in the town a lot of a Saturday night. I used to go in the NAAFI before I left and meet the lads and buy a round before leaving. The lads were alright, usually the heavy mob, but alright with it.

And I went in this night and there was lovely quiet lad there – a doctor's son called Jeff – who was saving up. Now I never had much, and we got talking and I asked him how much he'd got to with his saving. He said he had two hundred pounds.

"That's great," I said. "I don't have a light but I really admire you." He said: "That's nothing, Brummie's got four hundred saved up."

Now this was illuminating because Brummie was one of those lads who would sit in the bar pretending he's spent all his money, and tap me for a drink. I don't mind anybody saving, but pretending he'd got nothing was not good. And I went in the NAAFI the following week and Brummie's there and he asks me to get him a drink, and I said: "I tell you what - I'll get you a drink when you've spent all your four hundred pounds.

"Why don't you draw some out and buy everyone a drink."

He went bright red and it didn't go down to well with the rest of the lads either, that he'd been getting drinks from.

So I don't think he liked me too much after that.

# 9. Going for Gold

THERE was a Major, I think, who was a bit of a bumbling soul, and we used to take the mickey out of him.

I watched him once coming back on his bike with his shopping in the basket, and he rode straight into one of the barriers, and shot over the top. Another day, we did a parade with visiting dignitaries watching, and he marched that fast that he nearly marched us into this huge tank transporter. So we thought we had good reason to have a laugh.

But it just shows you how wrong you can be about a person, because I noticed that he wore a small blue ribbon, as did our Sergeant, and I asked the Sergeant what it was for. He said it was for Korea, and he went on to say that the Major was a hero, and that he called fire to save some Americans, but had called it close to his own position, and only a few of them had got out. I felt so ashamed, because here was a man who was ten times the man I was.

It's amazing how patriotic you become when you're abroad. I found myself standing up for being British in a German bar, when one of the local policemen, who were all armed, started loudly referring to us as 'British Babies.'

He went on to expound about the virtues of the German race. So I stood up, and as I could speak German, I said: "We're British and we're not babies. But how come it was the British babies who defeated you lot then."

Luckily it was all quietened down, but I thought it was worth saying.

Bob and I used to go out and try and attract the women and unfortunately German women knew that the Americans were the ones with the money, not us. We used to go out on the town with these phoney Amercian accents with a bunch of keys as though we had a car, and try to chat the girls up. We'd keep it up until we got outside, and after a bit of walking around pretending to look for the car, we'd have to admit we were British. We'd get nowhere but we had a bit of a laugh with it.

Now I've mentioned before that we had a lot of very tall buildings in that camp, and we were talking about one thing and another, and someone said: "I wonder if you could jump out of the top window."

I said: "I would if it was on fire." But obviously this must have stuck in my brain, because some time later we had come back from the pub, somewhat the worse for wear, and I decided to climb out and onto the ledge.

Paddy, who I'd joked with earlier over helicopter training, saw me and shouted: "Don't do it Charlie, it's not worth it!"

He thought I was committing suicide! I said it was okay, but I crawled down and dropped quite a way off the ledge. I was lying on the grass, a bit bruised because it was quite a way, and this officer comes along and asks the others who that man is on the grass.

"It's Landsborough Sir," came the reply, to which the officer said: "Where's he come from?" So they pointed upwards and he said "Damn Fool. Take him back up." And I said "Yeah, I'll have a proper go this time." But it was a stupid thing to do and they left me where I was.

The army opened my eyes to a number of characters, and proved to me that people could quite often surprise me. I first met Ron Thomas, for example, in the band The Rock Avons – he was the bass player, and was mentioned to me by the other lads who referred to him as 'Mary Thomas'. Now you couldn't get anyone less likely to be called Mary than Ron – he was very much one for the girls, and would do anything to get a crowd going. Then there were other characters, who you thought you knew but would suddenly surprise you, like the quiet Scotsman, who was always neat and tidy and never drew any attention to himself, but who suddenly disappeared only to be found gun-running years later.

Other characters would suddenly go missing, and the officer in charge would later receive postcards from South America or wherever, saying: "Wish You Were Here."

I was working with this lad in the stores one time and he suddenly said: "Can I tell you something? You're a complete failure." And I was a bit taken aback by this and I said: "What d'you mean?"

He said "Well look at you, you've got a good education, you can sing, and play guitar, you're a good athlete, and you're still in here doing the same job as me, on the same money as me, and I've got no education, and no talents, but I'm more of a success than you."

And he really impressed me with that because he wasn't saying it in a nasty way, he was just trying to shake a bit of life into me. And he was right.

We were moved to the town of Celle – we had a large camp nearby, and I joined a new band called The Onions – that's a great name for a band isn't it?

I was coming to the end of my days in the army – I had a bit of a reputation for being against authority and the officers were often having conversations as to how they could get rid of me. So they then put out a call for who wanted to do cross-country.

Now they didn't know that I'd ever done anything sporty, so I said: "I'll have a go at that." They took us out in the country, it was very cold, and I was warmly dressed, with tracksuit and jumper on, and I took the lead. I lost it about three times through losing direction, but at various points there were officers monitoring the progress and you should have seen their faces – the shock and surprise when they saw me in the lead. "Well done Landsborough, well done."

I could really run in those days, and there was a Sergeant who ran for the British Army, with all his finery on and running gear, and he was about two hundred yards behind me as I eventually ran through the gates to the camp. As I came through the gates, Tanner Jones, one of my mates from Birkenhead, was in the prison block – he was always in there for minor misdemeanours like staying out a bit too late – and he saw me and he shouted "Go on Scouse!"

I ran around the track, and I was tempted to stop and do a 'Loneliness of the Long Distance Runner' stunt and stop before the end, but I wanted the glory too much, so I sailed over the line.

The officers were absolutely amazed, and they had to give me some sort of praise.

After that they were putting a football team together and again I said I'd have a go, and we won, about 4-0, with me scoring two of them. One was a bit flukey, I had my back to the goal and I backheeled it – dead jammy. But these officers were amazed that this layabout had proved to be reasonably good sporting-wise.

The next sporting opportunity that came our way was boxing, and I kept my hand well down – I don't like getting punched at all – but my friend little Taffy put his hand up. I said: "What are you doing?" "Well I've done a little bit," he said, and I admired him for that.

He went to training every day, and he was sparring with this other Welsh bloke, a corporal who nobody liked, and I asked him how he was getting on and he said: "Oh I'm getting well battered. I can't get at him at all he's too good."

I said: "Can't you land a good one on him for all of us?" So he said he'd do his best and he came back after the next bout with a big smile on his face. So I said: "Did you get him Taff?"

"I got him. And d'you know how?" And he told me that they were sparring and this guy's head guard slipped down over his nose, and he put his hand up to move it and before he could stop him, Taffy got a punch in on his nose.

Taffy apologised and said he couldn't stop himself. But he got him.

As you can see by looking at me, I like long hair and I tried to grow it as long as I could. But the Sergeant Major who was a little stocky fella wouldn't have it and sent me off to the civilian barbers to get my haircut. The girl in there only took a bit off, but when the Sergeant saw it he said: "I thought I told you to get your hair cut. Go and get it cut properly!"

So I went back, but once again got the girl to take just a little bit off. Well I ended up getting three haircuts, until I ended up with the same cut as everybody else.

And I said to the Sergeant, who you could have a bit of a laugh with: "When I get out I'm going to grow my hair down to my shoulders," which I did of course, "and I'm going to come back here and stand at the gate and shake it at you."

# 10. The Washroom Blues

IN the army we used to have to go on these schemes in the middle of the night where we were supposed to be simulating war conditions.

You'd suddenly get this signal – I forget what it was – and have to dash out and get in your position in the wood. Each would have a number and you'd have to call it out.

Let's say I would be number seven – you'd hear the previous six numbers called out from behind bushes and trees, and then there'd be a silence when it came to number seven.

I was going through this period where I was falling asleep all the time. I'd have climbed up into some camouflage netting and I'd be sound asleep.

I even once curled up asleep on the back of this wagon, lying in a heap in the darkness and this officer sent the wagon off to get provisions and when they were loading, they kept stepping over this shadowy lump, until the officer said: "What's that?" and they found me, asleep.

I don't know what it was, and it only lasted for a couple of weeks or so but I was definitely a bit of a Rip Van Winkle.

The officers didn't particularly like me because I was a bit of a rebellious character I suppose.

So when we went on a scheme they used to give me the job of digging the latrines, which used to cause hilarity among the lads to see me disappearing into the wood with a spade and all the paraphernalia I needed, and they used to call me the RSM – and I'll let you guess what the S stood for – Regimental s*** Mechanic.

I can remember thinking I couldn't be bothered digging the three holes I was supposed to dig and I left the third one. Of course, when it came time to dismantle it, everyone had used the wrong one, which didn't make it a pleasant job to dismantle. But it was my own fault really.

And when I was setting one up, this officer came down and there's nothing more disconcerting than sitting on the toilet and having someone talking to you. I had this canvas screen round but his head was peering over the top.

He carried on a conversation with me, and it was embarrassing. And he waited for me to finish, and then he used it, and I was tempted to pop my head round and see how he liked it. But it was not one of my glorious jobs – RSM.

I used to have my guitar with me everywhere I went in the army.

The lads used to watch me and I'd sing for about an hour or so, and I'd feel miles better once I'd sung.

I'd go into the washrooms because we got a great echo in there. The nice thing is that 40 years later I bump into some of those lads and it's great to see them again. I remember little Paddy Weir from Northern Ireland – he used to hear me in the washroom – I think I was playing *Roll Over Beethoven* and he would say: "You should be doing something. You should be performing somewhere."

It's marvellous that I bump into him now, all these years later, and he's a great friend of mine.

Then there was Kenny Cummings from Scotland – I went looking for him when I got this break and I started playing around Scotland.

I was playing in Kirkcaldy and I looked for him everywhere in the town that day. As he was a bit of a lad for the ale – well we all used to drink too much – I was looking at all these down and outs thinking he must have got into a rough state by now.

I couldn't see him anywhere – I asked after him. And I was playing later, doing a little bit on my own, playing with my pedals, and I said: "One of my best friends came from this town. But knowing the way he used to drink he's probably dead by now." And this voice said: "Ah no, Charlie, I'm still here."

I couldn't see because the lights were dark, but in the interval they turned the lights up and there he was. He looked great, and my missus said to me: "You've got a cheek, he looks better than you. He looks like Elvis Presley." It was great to see him looking so well and married with children of his own.

I keep bumping into lads from then, all over the UK. When I left the army, Kenny told me that I said to him: "Look for me in music."

Now that sounds a bit arrogant to me, but if that's what I said – that's what I said. He said: "I've been looking for you ever since. You didn't half take your bloody time."

I remember when I was due out of the army – I'd saved up £200 to buy my way out – I'd got half way a number of times, I'd served four years, and I'd got fed up a number of times with haircuts and authority and everything.

I'd get halfway, and then I'd get fed up and I'd take the lads out on the town and I'd start again another time. But eventually I saved the money up, and I was due to go out in a day or two. I went out on the town, and on the way back there was a Luftwaffe display with a fence around it with armed guards on it. As a bit of bravado, I got into the camp, and I grabbed these ladders and climbed up and took armfuls of bunting.

As I was leaving this little camp this German saw me and shouted for me to halt. I ran off in a zig-zag, expecting to have bullets fly over my head. In the morning there was this bunting all over the camp and it was stupid, because it could have stopped me getting out.

A few days later I did get out and it's funny because you're saying

'Goodbye' to these lads who you've lived with for years, and these big fellas have got tears in their eyes telling me: "Look after yourself Scouse, won't you mate?" But that's the sort of bonds you make.

In Civvy Street you can meet people once a week and think they're great, and perhaps they are, but in the army you're with somebody day and night. And you know who the cheats and the liars are, and who the nice ones are and the generous ones, and you try to associate yourself with them as much as you can, or at least I did, and thankfully made great friends from my army life. I absolutely loved Germany – I think it's a beautiful country – the scenery's fantastic and I love the individuality of the towns. There seems to be a bit of character there compared to the housing estates we have here.

We had a bit of leave but didn't have much money, so me and a mate decided to go to the autobahn and thumb a lift. When the first lorry stopped, the driver asked where we were going and I said: "Where are you going?"

He said he was going to Hamelin so I said we'd go there. We just wanted to go anywhere. And we got to Hamelin – a beautiful place with lovely little narrow streets and quaint buildings and because it was nice and warm during the day we decided to sleep by this little pier on the river – we had ordinary sleeping bags. Then we woke up damp and freezing but it didn't really spoil the trip, I think the next night we slept in a cornfield.

We went into a pub and this German spotted us and came over – he saw the English cigarettes, which he was after, and he said: "Good Evening. I speak a very little English."

We asked him to sit down and we bought him a drink, and a few minutes later he repeated the same phrase, and then he repeated it again, a few minutes later. So he was right he did speak a very little English. Extremely little English, but it was good fun and we had a nice little break in the Pied Piper town of Hamelin.

# 11. Chicago Sect Appeal

ONE experience that really can't be missed out is the German Experience, if you like.

After I'd left the army I got a call from Ron Thomas, a bass player that I had played with, and he said: "Charlie we want a singer."

He'd been playing with a band in Dortmund. So he said: "Will you come?" I said yes. Now I was supposed to be going off to make some money to get married with. I left home with virtually nothing, and we hitched our way to Dortmund, and I arrived with just a couple of bob.

We met up with the rest of the lads in this band, who I didn't know, and they started firing questions at me like: "Do you know any Tamla?"

I said no, and in fact just about every question they asked I had to say no to because I'd been sitting in the pubs back in Merseyside singing Country and Western stuff, and they were like a pop band.

I was beginning to think this was terrible, and they were looking at the bass player as if to say: "What the hell have you brought him for?"

Then when all seemed lost, and I thought I was going to have to hitchhike all the way back from Dortmund with nothing, they asked if I knew any Ray Charles.

I said I knew Georgia and they said: "Oh, ok then, give us that." (I discovered afterwards that the guitarist had just learnt it.)

So I sang the song and that was it – they said: "You're in."

They gave me a whole pile of songs and said: "Learn all these by Saturday." This was something like Monday, and I had to know them all by the weekend, plus where all the intros and breaks were, so it was nerve-racking, but I was in the band.

It was the beginning of a lovely little episode, if you like, all sorts of things happening. I was in the band and we were away and running.

But I virtually had nothing. I think one of the first nights I was there, I had about 10 German Marks. And it was rough where we were – it was the brothel area really, but we were just down there having a pint.

We went into this bar – me with my 10 Marks – and I went up and ordered three beers, thinking it wouldn't be much, and the two girls behind the bar called out: "And a drink for us?"

But I had to say: "No, sorry love, that's all I've got.

"If I come in again and I've got money I'll buy you a drink but that's all I've got now."

They came over with the three beers and they gave me virtually no change. So I said: "What's this? We've only had three beers?" And she said "And the two drinks for us."

I said: "I didn't order two drinks for you," annoyed by this time, "That's all I've got in the world, I can't have that."

They weren't going to give me the change, so I said: "I want to see the Boss."

I was losing my temper, but then in the middle of all this, this chap walked in – an old drunk – and they were all ridiculing him, which I didn't like, and it was making me even more angry.

The old fella went to the bar and the two girls asked him if he'd like a drink and he nodded his head and she filled a glass full of water and she threw it all over him, and they all laughed at him. I thought that was just awful and I exploded – I was pushing my luck really – and I said: "Thank God I'm English" – the old patriotism was coming out again – "I couldn't see an Englishman ever doing something like that, you lot should be ashamed of yourselves."

By this time these heavies had lined up behind me – people had been killed in this area and these were gangsters – real heavies.

But luckily Ron knew them, through playing in the area, and he spoke to them and said: "Ah leave him, he doesn't know, he's new here. We'll look after him, leave him alone."

Thank God he did because they'd have killed me. Anyway they got me out of the place and a couple of weeks later I was playing with the band in this club.

I walked in there and those two barmaids were in the corner. I looked across at them in disgust and next thing this beer is sent over to me, and the barman says that it's off the two of them.

I don't know whether they were feeling ashamed of what they'd done that night so I forgave them. But it wasn't a nice area to be in and I think the first time I went into this club we played in, the lads introduced me to this fella called Manfred – he was a big burly soul and a hard case and they said: "This is Charlie."

I said hello and I had a beer in my hand and he said: "Can I have a drink of your beer?" I said: "Of course you can," and I gave him it and he took it, stared at me and drained the glass. Then he put it down and smiled. The lads laughed nervously.

I said: "You know you're a big man, but you're a very ignorant man, and what you've just done, well, I don't like it all."

And he smiled and he bought me a drink and said: "I like you."

It wasn't really a very good or auspicious start to my bookings in there, but then he liked me after that. He was just seeing what sort of character I was, I suppose.

When I was in the band with Ron Thomas we stayed in some really strange places, and for a while we stayed at the back of the one Wilhelmshof bar. We slept on a stone stage. There was a big hall at the back of this bar that was always empty, apart from when bands played. Otto, the lovely old guy who ran the place, used to let me and Ron sleep on the stone stage, which was uncomfy as you can imagine, especially if you're a bony person like me.

At night time obviously all the lights were off, and if you needed to get up to go to the toilet you'd have to negotiate your way through in the dark and the cold. We'd try to time it so we'd both go together, with one in front and the other behind – the idea being that if one fell, the other would be alright.

We were getting washed in the gentlemen's toilets, which weren't the best. The water was cold and we were hungry all the time.

Otto called us to say his wife had prepared us some food – we were delighted and went down, and his wife put this silver salver in front of us. When we lifted the lid off there was a whole fish, with the head and eyes and everything.

We couldn't eat it but we couldn't let him know, so when they weren't looking I took the whole fish and we left the room and dropped the fish in a bin outside. We'd have been happy with just a hunk of bread we were so hungry, but we couldn't eat that fish.

Another time Otto took us to a restaurant, but didn't ask us what we wanted to eat, and we ended up with oysters, which I hate. But I ate them all I ws so hungry.

But there was one place that we used to go where they knew exactly what we wanted and we'd walk in and they'd say "Omelette?" which would fill you up and was cheap.

We actually stayed in a farmhouse, with a tatty old freezing room, and for weeks we lived off a dish that Ron cooked, which was rice and raw eggs, sprinkled with a bit of cayenne pepper.

The room had mice, and I used to feed one of them, until I was having a cup of coffee and as I drained it I found mouse droppings at the bottom of the cup. And that ended my friendship with the rodent.

The band that I was playing in at the time was called the Chicago Sect and the teenagers loved us because we were an authentic British band and we were good – we played well, in fact the guitar player is still there, he's got his own band and he's had a great career.

We used to get full houses wherever we went – we didn't make very much money although I think the bar and club owners did – but we had a great time doing it.

When we weren't playing ourselves we would go down to this dodgy area to watch the other British bands that would come over.

I felt sorry for those lads because they would come from all over the British Isles, lured by the promise of touring Germany, which doubtless sounded very glamorous, only to find that the reality was they would end up playing a different place every night, they'd always have to chase payment, and they'd be staying in very rough accommodation.

I thought our farmhouse was bad, but I missed the bus back to ours one night, and ended up staying with one of the visiting bands in a farmhouse with no windows in, no heating, and one mattress between four or five. I did feel sorry for them.

We developed our own signature refrain when I was with the Chicago Sect, and it was flattering for us because it soon caught on with the other bands who would pick up on this, and before long all the bands were using the same little riff to end their sets. So we had them all following us around trying to learn what we knew.

Another place we stayed in was the attic of one of the buildings in the army camp where nobody ever went – the lads hid us away up there – and of a morning they would each smuggle a bit of breakfast for us. Then when they were all out on parade, Ron and I would sneak out, and then sneak back in again. We did that for a number of weeks. I had my hair longer at this stage, and sometimes the officers would be staring over from a distance, and you could see them trying to make out what it was they were seeing.

One morning we had come down for a wash, me with my beard and long hair and Ron looking equally odd, and this new lad, who'd only recently arrived in the camp, came in and saw us. He thought we must be soldiers and he was looking at us in amazement, and asked us: "What's it like here?" To which I answered: "It's fantastic, it's really laid back here and so relaxed."

Was he in for a rude awakening, if he believed that. But we didn't stay there too long – we realised we were pushing our luck. We went to this Pole who worked in the camp and lived in one of the apartment blocks, and it was immaculate. We paid him, which helped him out, but it was so rigid. He lived very frugally and went mad when Ron boiled a kettle.

One night we had been out, and we were a bit the worse for wear because we'd had a good night, and we couldn't get the key in the door for some reason, and before I could tell him not to, Ron had forced the key and snapped it in the lock. The poor old Pole was going mad – he was that worked up about drawing attention to us.

So needless to say we had our bags packed the next day. But I felt so sorry for him, he didn't have much.

I've said that I've never ever taken any drugs, but that's not completely true because when we were in Germany one of the lads in the camp had got these tablets, from the chemist, and they were called AN1s.

"Have one of these they're smashing," he said, and I took one and I felt fantastic, but they were meant for people with severe debility I think.

Now I love everyone generally when I'm in a good mood, but when I'd had this tablet I loved everybody ten times over, and I just wanted to put my arms around the world. They affected everybody differently, and I only took them for about two weeks, because I realised that it wasn't such a good thing to be doing.

It was marvellous for me, but one of the lads went walking around with his eyes really wide open like saucers and unable to speak.

They were good for the lads that wanted to go out of a night, and then be able to go out driving on a scheme the following day. But no, it wasn't a good thing to be doing – I stuck with them for about two weeks, but it wasn't right.

I've had some near misses during the course of my life, and one of them was in Germany when we were staying in the farmhouse.

Ron came in and said: "Quick get your guitar, and come down to this fancy nightclub, there's Rolls Royces and all sorts there, there's film cameras and everything, there's a talent competition on and everybody's there."

I couldn't be bothered, and he was really annoyed and he had every right to be annoyed, but I said no. And the following week – it was on every week – I agreed to go. We went down and won the prize of a bottle of champagne. The boss of the place came over to us and said: "Where were you last week – you would have romped it. I was one of the judges and you would have walked it. And the prize was a recording contract, and so many television appearances."

Ron was going mad. Instead we won one bottle of champagne which we finished in about fifteen minutes – one bottle doesn't go far between two. A great missed opportunity and I could have kicked myself later.

The other missed opportunity in Germany came when I was coming to the end of my stay and I was going back home – I got married to Thelma between times but I left her for a few nights because I'd promised the lads that I would go back. I said I wouldn't be gone for long.

Before I was due to come home, this German lad said: "Come on, jump in the car and let's go down to Ariola Studios in Cologne and lets have a last try at that."

So we said okay and put our guitars in, and he drove us to Cologne, which was a long way.

He went in ahead of us to the recording studios and persuaded the manager that he had to hear these guys from Britain.

So the manager eventually agreed, and he told him to wait until that particular recording was over and the red light had gone off, and then bring us in.

We went in, and the guy put a couple of mics in front of us, and I was so disappointed, I thought this just doesn't sound right at all, because we'd got no effects, it was just like sitting in your own room and singing. We sang two songs – the manager had obviously just decided to let us sing a couple of songs and then tell us to beat it.

Anyway I was packing up the guitar and the engineer said: "Hang on," and he went and got two fellas – one was a little fat fella with a big cigar looking like something out of an old rock and roll film – and when they played it back it sounded great.

I could see these guys nodding approval, and the engineer asked if I could speak German, and when I said yes, he asked me to go back and record a single for the German market. So I said: "What about Ron?" and he said, "Oh no, we've got plenty of bass players already."

So I said: "Well I'm sorry but no, he's responsible for me being here, and if he's not in it I can't do it."

He said: "Alright, you and your friend." So I went outside and I said: "We've cracked it Ron, we're going to make a record!"

And we drove back in high spirits all the way to Dortmund.

I came back home shortly after, and as usual I was skint and the only one who had any money at all was our Arthur. I thought he'd be able to lend me the money to go back there. But Arthur had fallen off his bike and broken his leg so he hadn't been working and didn't have the money. So that was it. I never got back to Ariola Studios and that opportunity went begging.

We had some nice fans in Germany, some of the lads were from very good families – well off, you know – and good people.

Two of these lads were going over to England and they wanted to go and see the Cavern, so they asked me if I knew anywhere they could stay. I wrote to my brother and asked him if he could put them up. And he wrote back and said yes, so they went over and had a great time.

Around Christmas time these two lads were writing a card, and they were putting money in it, and they said: "Do you know who this for? It's for your brother Arthur, and some for Jack. If all Englishmen are like your brother it must be a wonderful place."

And I thought that was a lovely thing for them to say.

What it was – Arthur had never taken a penny off them for putting them up and feeding them, and Jack had taken them round to get their vehicle mended when it went on the blink, and they took them to see the cavern, and never took a penny off them.

Before they left, Arthur gave them some money, and this was the money they were sending back. They were very taken with him, and with their experience.

While I was in Dortmund, we weren't playing, and I went about looking for my friends. I was in the rough area, and I bumped into these two German lads, or they bumped into me. I said sorry, and they said: "Sorry Grandad?" I had my beard of course – and they pushed me into the corner. I said: "Yes I'm sorry, I didn't mean it."

I thought I'm going to get battered here, I'll have to hit one of them and go down fighting. And just when it all looked ominous, this door opened and there was Johnny Porter, who I hadn't seen in years since Celle, and he was a big lad, Johnny. "Scouse!" he said and the two Germans took one look at this six-foot-three fella and turned on their heals and beat it. "It's great to see you Scouse," said Johnny. "You've no idea how great it is to see you Johnny," I replied. "You've just saved my life."

He took me inside and all the lads were there who I hadn't seen for years. We had a great time – so much so that when they were trying to give me a lift home – by this time they had got me absolutely blotto – they quickly realised that I didn't know where I was, or where I lived, so they took me back to the army camp and covered me up with a blanket in one of the rooms.

The officer found me the next morning and didn't know what it was he was uncovering, seeing this great hairy thing underneath the blanket.

And you can imagine the language, I had to be got out of there pretty quickly. But he saved my bacon, Johnny Porter, that night.

# 12. Sent to Coventry

WHEN I'd left the army I was living in Beaufort Road on my own.

I didn't have a job at the time and my brother Arthur used to come around and put food in the larder and leave a ten bob note on the cabinet, and he never condemned me.

While I was living there, two ex-army colleagues of mine – Tony and Kenny – came over to see me. They were on the run, and were both skint, and they ended up staying with me. Thelma used to bring a dinner round from her mam's – we weren't married then – and I'd share it three ways.

One morning a policeman came up the path and the two of them panicked and shot off. I opened the door and he said: "Charles Alexander Landsborough . . . " Well it turned out he was passing a message for my dad, but it scared the life out of them.

We knew that one of us would have to get a job, so I borrowed sixpence off my sister for the phone because we'd seen a driving job and Kenny could drive – I couldn't and Tony couldn't. We phoned up and Kenny got the job, so that's brilliant, we thought.

Kenny set off on the Monday – I got him up like a Dad – and come Friday when it was his pay day we were looking forward to being taken out for a few pints. Probably a bit cheeky since he'd done all the work, but we'd looked after him.

And when he came in he had his share of our little bit of food, he got washed, put his good clothes on, and then went out on his own.

We sat there, mouths open, but we thought maybe he'd take us out Saturday. But come Saturday, the same routine happened and it began to dawn on us that Kenny wasn't going to take us out at all.

And he didn't. And I felt like strangling him because we'd always shared everything. But it was sad about Kenny, because he emigrated to Canada, and came back once to see us, but just after going back he was mowed down in a hit and run accident, and he was killed. He was a great character, God bless him.

Another time I was sitting in the house on my own and another old army pal, Jimmy Butler, pulled up outside in a wagon. We had a little talk and I said I was going down to Coventry on the Monday.

"There's plenty of work down there," I said, "and I'm going to get a job in the car factory."

"Hang on," Jimmy said "If you let me pack my job in I'll come with you." So he did, and off we tootled down to Coventry – he had a couple of bob and I had absolutely nothing.

I thought we'd get jobs in the car industry, make a fortune and everything would be fine. But when we got down there, you couldn't get a job in the car industry anywhere, they were all full up. Jimmy could drive, which I still couldn't do, and he got a job as a tyre fitter I think.

We stayed in this house, courtesy of Jimmy, and the landlady didn't like me very much because she saw him working and me doing nothing so she just thought I was lazy. So we left there and we got a place in the Stoke Hill Guild House, which was where you went if you didn't have much – all sorts of characters finished up there.

I didn't have the money to go there and I'd walk the streets to the dole office only to wait ages and be told I was in the wrong place, and I'd have no money for fares so I'd walk off again. And I walked miles to this other place and eventually I was told that they couldn't give me anything.

I was desperate and I'd seen others get money ahead of me, so I told them they'd have to have me forcibly ejected because I wasn't leaving. Finally they gave me the four pounds to pay for a room in the Guild House. And we stayed there for a couple of weeks.

The only place I ended up getting any work was the Post Office. The post people were nearly all women, but I got a job there. It was very hard work and it meant getting up very early in the morning but I liked it because you were out in the fresh air. When we were training I made friends with an Irishman and a West Indian.

I was sitting on the bus in my uniform, and the bus conductor kept passing me asking for any fares, but I kept quiet until she eventually confronted me and I said: "Postman, love." She said: "Even postmen have to pay when they're on their way to work."

So I said "I've got no money at all."

And she just shrugged and tutted and stormed off and I felt inches tall, because everyone was turning round to see who this bum was who had no money. But it was such a long way to work that I sat it out.

When I went for the test, they gave us an English test and a Maths test. I finished the maths but I romped through the English test, so I had loads of time left. This lovely African lad next to me was struggling, so I filled in some of the answers for him. At the end the examiner told me I'd passed, and he said to the African guy, who couldn't speak much English, "Your maths wasn't very good but your English was excellent. That must really be your strong point." And the poor chap tried to answer him but couldn't speak English, and the examiner looked at him, then looked at me with suspicion, and he didn't get the job.

So we had a break in the canteen, and I had just about enough money for a cup of tea, and I was watching people around me eating bacon and eggs, and I was starving. This other lovely lad, a West Indian called Alfie Hinds, asked: "Aren't you eating Charlie?"

When I said no he must have realised because he handed over a couple of bob and said: "Go and get yourself something." I could have kissed him. And I got my bacon and eggs.

We used to put a bet on, of a Saturday, and two of the lads, Alfie and an Irishman, went into this betting shop, but I didn't fancy the limits. "What are you on about?" they said, "When are you likely to win?"

I remember this one time I'd had three winners and a non-runner, and I was looking in the paper and there was this horse called Eyes Down. Now, there was a fella used to sit with us who was always asking me to come down the bingo with him. So when I saw his horse I backed it, and it came in at a hundred to eight.

To this day, I remember that I won one hundred and forty seven pounds fifteen and three. And I took the other two lads to the betting shop and we picked up my winnings, which was like £1000 these days. I took the lads out and I bought a pair of jeans for myself and an engagement ring for Thelma.

But I never forgot walking the streets, before I had the postman's job, with only enough for a cup of coffee in my pocket.

I'd walk and walk, to pass the time and then stand in a doorway by a café and think, "I'll wait until half eleven and then I'll go in" and when half eleven came I'd wait a bit more, and then go in for a cup of coffee. I'd stay in the warmth with it until it got embarrassing, because I'd only have enough for the one cup, and then leave.

And I was standing in this doorway when this old Irish fella came up and asked if I'd like to buy a copy of Old Moore's Almanac, so I said: "I'm sorry Paddy, me old mate, I've only got a tanner."

He walked on, then turned and came back and said: "Here you go, fella," and he gave me a copy and said, "Any man from Dublin is a friend of mine," so I had a great impression of the Irish long before I ever got there.

Not long after I'd won the money, I got my first week's wages, and I was out in the town, and this little Irish fella came over and said: "Have you got the time please?"

I said: "Yeah, Paddy it's up on the clock there look," and when he heard the accent his eyes lit up and he said "Scouse! You couldn't lend us two bob could you?"

I said no, but I walked him over to the pub and I bought him four batches and a couple of pints, and he'd walked about fifteen miles that day. I got such pleasure out of that because he was in exactly the same position that I'd been in a week or so before.

When we finished I asked him where he was staying that night, and he didn't have anywhere, so I took him back to our place, and put him in the little drying room which was really warm, and I gave him a little ticket for his breakfast in the morning.

But it was great to see his face and to think of the situation I'd been in the previous week.

When I'd just started my job in the post, I came back to the room one day and there was Jimmy packing his case, and he blushed when he saw me. So I asked him what he was doing and he said: "Oh I'm going, I've met this girl and I'm staying with her in Nuneaton." And I said: "That's ok Jim, you don't need to be embarrassed – I'd have done the same thing myself."

He ended up marrying that girl – I've had a hand in a few weddings along the way, introducing people to each other.

Sadly, when I won the money, he'd gone and I never saw him or his girl, which was a shame because he'd been good to me. But I did hear about his wedding in Nuneaton.

In the Post Office there were a lot of Asian workers, and Irish and a lot of women. The boss came over to me one day and asked if I wanted any overtime, so I said yes. I went over to Alfie and asked him if he was doing it because he had loads of kids and he needed the money, and he said no, he wasn't asked.

So he went and asked the boss about it and he was told no.

I went over and asked the boss why he didn't ask Alfie and he looked a bit embarrassed and said that when the Asian boss was on he used to give all the overtime to the Asian lads and leave the English out. So he retaliated by only offering the overtime to the English.

I said: "Poor old Alfie will never get any overtime because he's not Asian and he's not English, and he needs it more than most."

So the boss gave in and Alfie got the job and I was delighted.

I liked being on the post because once you'd got your stuff together you could work on your own, but you did also meet some odd characters. My area was the Hipswell Highway in Coventry and one fella kept coming out asking if there was anything for him and I'd say no and he'd keep coming out and I'd keep telling him there was nothing for him. He was almost accusing me of keeping something from him, but eventually he got what he was waiting for.

But that was a bit strange.

I had a variety of jobs after that, until I was back working at the gas board as a labourer, chipping away at a pipe in a hole in the depth of winter, and I was freezing. I thought, there's got to be something better than this.

I was talking to a lad down the pub later who was a teacher and he suggested trying that: "You've had a good education why don't you try teaching?"

# 13. I'd Like to Teach the World to Sing

I APPLIED to be a teacher and I was amazed when I got a letter inviting me to go in for an entrance exam for mature people.

I was even more amazed when I passed and was invited to join the course. I was a little bit afraid because I'd just come from labouring and I was going to be with all these clever people, and I thought I'd look out of place.

I remember talking to the vicar at the time and he told me that lovely tale about the priest who was approached by a man who arrived in the town, and asked him what the people there were like.

The priest asked what they were like where he'd been and the man said they were horrible, and he couldn't wait to get away from them.

The priest said: "Well they're just like that here."

The man went away and the next day another man approached the priest and asked the same question, and the priest again asks what the people were like where he'd been and he said they were marvellous.

Again the priest says: "Well that's what they're like here."

What my vicar was saying to me was that I'd be alright wherever I went as long as I treated people well.

So I went to the course, and the transformation was quite traumatic because on the Friday, I'd been drilling concrete and there's nothing worse when you're a thin fella, I was shaking about all over the place. On the Monday I was sitting in the college listening to Mozart and I thought this is great. I had three years training and by this time our Jamie had been born, and he cried all night during my first teaching practise – they threw you in at the deep end. I'd only been at the college a few months and I was out doing teaching practise, trying to take notes and prepare lesson plans while the baby's crying – it was a pretty stressful time actually, but I survived and got through it.

My great friend in teacher training college was Jimmy McGovern – the wonderful writer and a lovely man, Jimmy.

I met lots of lovely people in there, and I was educated. I started off in the Theology department because I'd found my faith by then and it was an eye-opener because I'd thought I would be surrounded by people who believed as I did, in a naive sort of way. But whenever I spoke up I was torn to shreds by the brilliant lecturer. I remember him asking: "Who believes in heaven?"

I said: "I do." And he looked at me in a very disparaging way and said: "What's it like then?" I said: "I don't know I just know that Jesus Christ is there and that's enough for me." And he looked at me with great disdain, and it wasn't a very pleasant experience being in the Theology department, but you were doing bits of other things, and I'd go into the music department, which I loved and was beginning to shine in, and they said to me: "What are you doing in the Theology department? You should be in here."

So I swapped, and it was the best thing I ever did. Mrs Hartley, and the other lady whose name escapes me would play me bits of classical music and ask me what I thought of it. I'd say "I don't like it . . . it's boring, there's no rhythm in it."

Slowly and surely bits began to get to me and I began to like it – there's still a lot I don't like, but they opened my eyes to musical ideas.

It became mind-boggling to see the mathematical beauty behind some of the work that Bach wrote. The same lady sent me off to write my own little pieces of music. Now I can't play the piano but I had a go and it was something fairly predictable I suppose, but I tagged a quirky little bit on the end.

She played this piece and nodded, then she came to the quirky little piece and she lit up. And she said: "This is the sort of thing I'm looking for," and carried on playing this little piece, which shot me off on a tangent, and I was writing more quirky little pieces of music.

I wrote a selection of pieces for a Transport theme with things like *Bike With A Bumpy Tyre*, and every so often this bass note would go up like a bump in the road and *Hot Air Balloon* which gradually disappeared up and out of sight – little odd things. The more inventive I was the more she liked it. When I finished up, you had to do this final piece of work and for mine I wrote six pieces of piano music, very painstakingly but I could work out what I liked slowly, and I incorporated the little musical tricks she had taught me into the pieces.

Some people had written huge tomes about music or composers and my compositions were really thin by comparison, and I handed it in almost apologetically.

But Mrs Hartley said: "Don't be sorry, Charlie, I'm a composer myself and I know the work that's gone into this."

She played it and the students gave me a standing ovation. I'd never heard this stuff until Mrs Hartley played it. It sounded great to me because it was the first time I'd heard it in its entirety.

So I have a lot to thank Mrs Hartley for – her son by the way was Bill Hartley the athlete.

Now I was pretty hopeless at playing anything other than the guitar, but they were doing a musical presentation in the music department and I was told by Mrs Hartley that I was playing the bass recorder. So I said to her: "Be it on your own head. I'll try my best but I'll be awful."

But she told me I'd be fine. I was the introduction to the piece with my solo effort on the recorder.

It was desperate, and looking around the audience you could see in the faces the suppressed laughter. It was awful but we had a good laugh about it all. It wasn't too bad once the other instruments joined in and drowned me out, but fancy giving me the solo introduction.

You couldn't have had a worse start to the evening. But she learnt her lesson from there I think.

At the Training College there were quite a few ladies of substance financially, and I was still a bit of a scruff. I had this pair of corduroy shoes, a bit like slippers, and they seemed to expand in the rain – they spread outwards. I remember running up the hill to college in the rain and I was absolutely soaked, and my feet were soaked, and my shoes looked awful.

When I got in I was trying to hide my feet under the seat, and I could see these ladies sitting opposite me staring down in disbelief at my shoes – and in particular this one lady who now lives just up the road from me. I suppose all that matters is that I did get through it and I did pass, and I don't think everybody did, in fact I don't think she did.

So I mightn't have had the right shoes but I did pass.

I went into training College in 1976, and I got my first job in 1978 I think it was. I applied for a job in Cavendish Street School in Birkenhead. There were a few applicants including Sue Smith, a lovely friend of mine, and one of my favourite people.

I went in and waited outside afterwards and Sue came out after and said she had the job. I was pleased for her because she was a lovely person but I thought I was up the creek, but then they called me back and gave me a job as well.

I finished up teaching for fourteen years. We were in Cavendish Street for a couple of years and then they moved us to the old Laird Street – the old school of Everton Football Club's legendary Dixie

Dean was its claim to fame – and it became Portland School.

They picked a street halfway between Cavendish Street and Laird Street and named the school after that to avoid anybody getting upset. It was a rough old school at times but we had some great laughs and it did me proud. I wrote a fair few songs while I was a teacher.

I wish I'd recorded all of the assemblies I did because they really did turn out good. I used to write usually a comic sort of script and I'd write a song to go with it and the kids were fantastic at doing things like that, they really were.

And the funny thing was, in Laird Street the staff had these anagrams which I'd made up out of their names, for example Doug Fallowes the head became Gus Lodawofle. I called someone else the Asthmatic Angel because you'd make her a cup of tea and she'd say: "Ahhhhhhhh bless you."

Quite a few of them had different names and during assembly I'd put these names in and the kids didn't know who was who. But the teachers did.

I remember having a class of thirty three or so in a very small room, and it was unbelievably difficult to say the least because everywhere you looked there was a problem, God bless them, one lad had seen his father hang himself, many had parents in jail for drugs or robberies, and the stress of just trying to keep order was immense, but at the same time I did have some laughs in that classroom.

One tale I always like is when I was teaching about the Roman calendar and I put these questions on the board after I'd told the kids what it was all about. One of the questions said: "Which month of the year used to be the eighth month of the year and which creature's name starts with the same three letters, an why do you think this is so called?"

And of course it was October and Octopus, and little Robbie came out, who wasn't the brightest lad, and he whispered to me and said: "I know that one Sir, it's an octopus isn't it?" I said "It is. Well done son. Keep it to yourself."

He came back to me having had a brain wave and whispered to me again: "And I know why it's called that Sir, it's 'cos it's got eight testicles."

And as he was walking back to his desk I thought "Don't draw a picture Robbie for God's sake."

It was very difficult at times because you'd see kids occasionally that weren't being looked after properly, or who were trying to be a mother to their siblings. And at times you'd think I'd like to take that little girl home and get Thelma to bath her and get her to look like she'd never seen herself looking like before.

But obviously you could never do anything like that. So it did have its hard side, but we did have some great successes.

We had a little girl called Nicola and she had a great brain on her, she was miles ahead of anyone else in her class.

Her brother was an absolute pain – it was hard to believe they came from the same family.

He finished up in a school for kids with behavioural problems, but she was lovely and I suggested that the parents put her in for the Birkenhead School, which is a very prestigious school to attend, because there were certain free places which were awarded, and she passed the test and got the place.

I said to her: "You may find girls there who are better off materially than you but they're no better than you love, you're every bit as clever as they are, just you remember that."

She came back in her uniform about four months later and she looked great. And I asked her what it was like and she said: "It's great, Sir." I thought that was brilliant because she will escape that poverty trap, and she had a bright future. I'd love to know where she is now, but I was delighted for Nicola.

Another little girl I taught was Pauline, who was the daughter of a lad I grew up with, and one day I was in the classroom and another girl said: "Hey Sir, Pauline's been stealing stuff out of your stockroom."

So I said: "Have you Pauline?" And she said: "No I haven't."

So I said that was alright and I never pursued it. But a couple of weeks later she asked to see me at the end of Assembly and I met her outside the classroom after all the other kids had shot off out into the playground. I had always told them that they could always ask to talk to me if they were worried about anything.

Pauline came to me and told me that she had been taking the paper out of the stockroom: "But I'll never do that again because I'm a Christian now," she added. So I said: "That's very courageous of you to say that. We'll forget all about it now. Well done." And off she went, I thought that was fantastic.

Another little girl came in with her mother to see me, while another child was waiting to have her work marked, and the mother said: "She says you're picking on her." So I said: "Well I'm sorry to hear about that, because I'd never pick on anyone, least of all a child.

"I do tell them off if they're not doing their work, because I want the best for them. I treat all children here exactly the same."

And the other lovely little girl who was waiting alongside said: "That's right Sir, you do Sir."

That same lovely girl is now a teacher at that same school. And the little girl who'd said I was picking on her shortly afterwards rushed up to me in the playground and hugged me.

So she knew I was only looking after her in the end. In fact I was going in one day and she was stood in the passageway – everybody else was in the classroom so I asked her what was wrong because she looked unhappy, and she said: "I don't want to go in Sir," and I said: "Neither do I love, come on we'll go in together." So she got to like me in the end.

There were some kids who you would have to battle with for months and months, and there was one boy who was a bit manic when he arrived, but he loved football. He'd throw a complete wobbler for no reason at all, so I would tell him that he would miss football practise and he hated that.

I told him: "Once you have learned to control yourself you can play football – it's only people who can control themselves that should be playing football."

It took months and months for him to get the message. I used to be going home at night and I'd see all the lads playing football, and there was this lad having to watch from the side and I felt terrible because I knew how much he loved it.

But gradually he came round, and I said to him: "If you feel you're going to explode just stop and think about it." And one day he came in with his mum, having run out of the school, and he was effing and blinding shouting: "I hate him!"

I said: "I'm very sorry to hear that but listen son, you're expecting special treatment and you're not on. If you misbehave I'm going to tell you off and you've got me until next June so you'll have to get used to me and I'm not going to change the rules to suit you. I want the best for you but I want you to behave yourself."

At the end of the year he was completely different – he nearly killed me in the process – and his mother came to me and said she could never thank me enough for what I'd done.

He turned out to be a smashing lad.

Not so long ago I received an email from the outback in Australia from this girl who I had taught all those years ago, and she said in it that I had made a huge impression on her back then, which I was totally unaware of and she just wanted to thank me.

She was a lovely girl and very bright. She said that she was teaching Aboriginals and that one of the Aboriginal mothers loved my music. So I contacted her and thanked her for the lovely email and I sent a CD off for the mother. It's amazing where you get fans from isn't it?

Teaching could also be very gratifying sometimes. We had streamed groups for those that were slower learners, which I thought was a good idea because then they would have a chance to shine in their own group. And there was a big tall girl who was lovely, and she was always coming over to me and passing me little notes saying I love you Sir. She was lovely.

When I got my big break in music, I went back to the school and they were filming me. I was singing in the middle of the playground with a lot of the kids around me, and one of the ex-pupils who was now a girl of about eighteen, was standing by the railings watching.

The producer said to her: "What was he like as a teacher? I bet he gave you a hard time." She said: "No, never in your life, he never had a bad bone in his body."

I thought that was lovely. She was a great kid and it was easy to be nice to her, but recommendations from kids like that is marvellous because we all know kids tell the truth.

I remember once dreading this inspection we were having, and I was aware that I wasn't very good at certain areas of teaching.

As a primary school teacher you are expected to be good at all subjects, but I did think I was good at teaching art and poetry and creative things.

They were great at poetry once I turned them on to it. The head inspector had been in during one of my poetry lessons, and I will confess that inspections made liars out because I would tick boxes for things that I hadn't done, because it would cause mayhem if you didn't and you couldn't possibly do all of the things that they expected you to do.

The following morning the inspector met me in the passageway and asked to have a private word. I thought I'd been found out.

The previous day it seemed that they had all been marking lessons they had observed and the inspector had said that he had enjoyed my poetry lesson.

So the Head told him that I was a singer/songwriter and he gave him a tape and they listened to it in the dinner hour, which I knew nothing about. This inspector told me that he loved the tape and that he thought I had a special talent. He ended up coming along to loads of gigs – I think he lived in Stoke somewhere, and if we were playing anywhere near that area you would see him in the front row.

So, thank God I didn't get caught out like I expected to.

I was always slightly mischievous and one day this big-wig came to teach us how to teach. It wasn't a teaching day and we all gathered in my classroom and sat at the children's desks. He was a bit of an officious type and he said: "I am going to show you how to take a lesson. History – The Vikings!"

He stood up in front of the class and he shouted: "I am Thor. I am Thor. I am Thor!"

I shouted back: "Well rub some Vatheline on it then," in a rather camp way.

The whole place erupted and I don't think he looked at me for the rest of the day. But it pricked his pomposity a little bit and we all had a bit of a laugh.

I remember Gus Lodawofle, or Doug Fellowes as he normally was, walking in cheerily humming: "bum bum bum bum b-bum."

Someone said: "He's cheerful." I said "No, he's just counting the staff."

At the end of the year when the children are all waiting to find out which class they'll be in the next year, and I remember this time they were all lined up and the announcement came "Class L will be going to Mr. Landsborough."

There was a big cheer which was a lovely feeling to have as a teacher. You know you've succeeded.

# 14. Great to be Good: About Faith

GOING back right to the beginning, I had my first encounter with my belief, when I was a lad at Primary school.

I had a teacher called Mr Peake and he told a story about Jesus Christ – little did he know the impact that it would have on my heart at that particular time. I thought it was fantastic, and I discovered that it was good to be good.

I lived in a rough area where there were petty fights and squabbles and you had to be a bit of a tough nut to survive, so it was fantastic to hear it was 'good to be good' and that I was going to live forever.

I came out of school feeling totally elated and that I had to do something for this Jesus Christ. There was this old fellow passing, and I was quite shy as a lad, but I said to him: "Can I carry your bag, please for you Mister?" And he smiled at me and said: "Ah, no son, I'm fine thank you but that's very kind of you, thank you."

And I ran home absolutely delighted with what I'd just discovered. I started to sneak into churches because of the feeling – I wanted to get closer to this thing that I'd just discovered, and my brothers, who were all marvellous people, discovered me reading these Holy books, and they sort of ridiculed me – I think it was Harry who said: "Have you seen what Holy Joe's reading here?"

I wasn't sort of strong enough mentally or any other way to resist this onslaught, and buried it for years. Well it wasn't so much an onslaught, but it was enough to put me off for years and years.

I'd even argue against it, particularly when I was in the army I became bitterly resentful, and I didn't want to go on church parades or anything. I argued against it but this thing kept nagging away at me all the time.

Years later, I was in a pub and I thought I had to go and hit somebody with these questions that nobody around me knew were still chipping away at me. And I thought I'll go in every church that I can find until I get one with somebody in.

From the Pacific pub all the way to Hoylake there's a long drag with a lot of churches. I thought, I'll keep going and go in every one until I find someone who's got something to say for themselves.

The first church I went into was the Catholic church, and although it was open there was nobody in. I sat there for about five minutes then I left and went to the next one which was St James's, which would have been my local parish church in the North End of Birkenhead. There was a bloke at the door who asked me what I wanted and I told him I'd like to speak to the vicar.

So the vicar came out and he asked me what it was I wanted to know and I said that I had a number of questions that I needed to ask him about. He said: "Well, I'm conducting a burial service in a moment, but if you come back on Friday to the vicarage I'll talk to you for as long as you like."

I said, "I'll admit I've had a couple of drinks but I mean what I say." He said: "Of course. See you on Friday."

Of course come Friday, I'd sobered up – well, I hadn't had that much to drink, but by then I hadn't had any at all and I really argued with myself whether I should go or not.

But eventually I forced myself to go and he brought me in – a lovely man – Mr Spurry, and I challenged him with these questions that had been eating away at me and he answered them all in such a kindly way. He was a very articulate and erudite man. I think he had a couple of degrees, clever but a really nice man as well.

He answered my questions and thoroughly disarmed me, so all the sort of anger disappeared and at the end of our meeting – we spoke for ages – he said: "Kneel down and we'll say a prayer."

I felt really indignant that he should ask me to say a prayer. But I knelt down, still feeling indignant, and afterwards when I left I felt really marvellous – better than I had done in years. All the rubbish that I had taken seemed to sort of disappear and I realised that so many things you are led to believe you should follow are rubbish.

And I felt that I was finally on the right path.

After that meeting Mr Spurry couldn't keep me away and I finished up getting baptised there in St James's and I used to help out at the Church. The lads down at the Pacific – I knew all the 'Del' boys, all the live off their wit characters – were saying to themselves that I'd gone round the bend and become a religious nut. But they said it was only a passing phase and I'd come out of it.

Thankfully, I never did and the passing phase still hasn't passed and many years have passed since. But they used to have a go at me – they'd have a real dig at me.

I remember after playing in the pub one Sunday someone said something and I said to them: "Listen why are you getting so mad?

"This Jesus that I believe in demands the very best of me. I don't want to hurt anybody. I don't want anybody's money or anybody's wife. I'm going to lead a good life, and be good to my wife and look after my kids and even if I fail that's what I'm attempting to do."

Slowly but surely they realised that this wasn't going to pass with me and they were great after that.

This change resurrection, if you like, took place when I was about thirty. I remember coming home from the church and, as usual, I was late and Thelma was used to me being late and would have a go at me and she said to me: "Where have you been till now?" I said: "You'll never guess. I've been to church."

She nearly fell over, you know, and that was the beginning of a huge transformation of me getting back to where I belonged, I suppose.

People say that faith is a belief and that it's a crutch for the weak. Well it's a funny old crutch because it doesn't half make huge demands on you. I say the hardest 'case' to have ever lived was the Good Lord, to have gone through what he went through for us.

There are huge demands and there is constant temptation that you have to resist. It's a very difficult path to tread but I've always striven not to be sanctimonious or judgmental of others and to be forgiving of others and hopefully they would be forgiving of me.

I've seen occasions when people are a bit self-righteous and puffed up from pride and hopefully the Good Lord will deliver me from that. So it's had a huge impact on me and the way I think and the way I act. And I hope it continues to do so. And although I've still got many faults I think the Good Lord's helped me overcome quite a number and I don't think – please God – that will ever change. I'll keep on following.

I've prayed ever since those days. I used to pray, like most of us probably do, selfishly, asking for things like a kid to his dad, you know – I think particularly with the music because I'd think, well he's given me this gift and I'd ask him to give me success.

In 1994 I became aware that it was not the right way to approach things, so I began to pray differently. I'd say: "Listen, Lord, you've given me these musical gifts, the best gifts that you could give me, and I play the best that I can, but everywhere I turn I face rejection, and although I'm enjoying playing in the pubs where I am, if I try to better myself and get on I seem to get a slap in the mouth.

"Alright, I give in if it's Your will, and you really want me to be a teacher in Birkenhead I will, but I don't fancy it, in fact – I hate it.

"So you'll have to help me out, big time."

And it's almost as if, from that spiritual submission, that the whole thing began to happen not long after that. I think it was the submission – he was waiting for me to say, "Your Will be done" and that was it.

In January 1995 I'd had another rejection, but I came away and phoned RTE in Dublin, asking would they have me on there. They invited me over and I went on just with an acoustic guitar and the bass pedals, and did a couple of songs. I think the Almighty was definitely there with me that night, because something magical happened for me. I never ever watched the programme – it was broadcast only in Ireland – but that was the beginning of this wonderful life that I've had since.

A number of years ago I started going to the Christian Centre which is a Pentecostal church. My nephew, John Landsborough came along – my son was there as well – but John came and he got really engrossed in the whole thing. My brother Jack, who never went to church, thought that he was getting into some kind of strange sect or something so he came along to see what was going on, and he finished up going himself.

Eventually we were all fully baptised – I'd been baptised with a sprinkling before that – but this was a full immersion and we were all baptised in that one place.

Thankfully Jack did that, because not long after he became ill and eventually died of lung cancer but he was thankfully saved before he died. I'd left him in hospital to go and play in Ireland, I'd kissed him and said goodbye to him. The day he died, he looked up as though he was looking to heaven, held his arms out wide, smiled and died. And I think the Almighty came for him.

Once I was in the pub and three of the local hard cases were there.

I didn't know them that well, but as I got up to go, this one who was a bit of a scrapper, said: "See you next week."

And I said: "Yes, God willing." And another of them said in a very nasty cynical way "God? Who's he?" And I said: "Oh he's here alright." And he looked at me in total disgust.

And the following week I think he found out because he was killed in a car crash. I shudder to think how he felt when he passed away.

I've never seen anything but good come from somebody finding the Almighty. I've seen so many other lives changed by submission to the will of Jesus Christ. And one of the most remarkable was my cousin Stanley. I used to try and get him because he was a severe alcoholic at the time and I'd try to talk to him about God but he wasn't the least bit interested, and he'd tell me to shut up.

But he came one night to the pub and asked me to get him a bottle of gin. Now I didn't have much money at the time and I couldn't afford it and I said: "Look, I'll buy you something to eat but I can't get you a bottle to help you to kill yourself."

He had an addiction to tablets that were like heroin or something on top of the drink and he was desperate and he said: "If you don't get it for me, Charl, I'll kill myself. I can't get through the night."

So I got him a bottle of gin and I said: "Stanley have you said your prayers?" He said: "Not now, Charl." And he went home and not long after he sent his wife out to borrow some money to get some drink and he sent her down to the off-licence and she came back with some Guinness and he cursed her because Guinness was like water to him.

So he drank that, and I think he even drank some after-shave to get him through the course of the night, because he thought that there was spirits in it. He spent the night seeing things and shouting to God and in the morning sent his wife out again to the off-licence to get some barley wine – the next best thing to spirits.

He cursed the church when he looked out of his back window because it blocked the view to the off-licence, because he wanted to draw comfort from seeing her with the cans in her hand. She came back and he tasted them and said they were off.

She tasted them and said they were fine. But that was the last drink he had. I've got a picture of him meeting the Queen in that very church. He changed as a person, and dropped the anger and became very affable, and helpful and honest. He'd ride around on his bike with his little dog. You could trust him with anything.

He'd been admitted into a drying out clinic on a Good Friday which was unusual, and months later I was talking to him about it and he said: "People say it's my will power, but that's not right. I haven't got any. It's Him upstairs. It's God that's done that for me."

The transition from the aggression into the mellowness took a few months but gradually he left all that bad side behind him.

Thank God.

Something unusual happened later. The power of prayer I guess.

I was playing in a pub on the Ford Estate with Kenny in the duo and we were in the middle of a song, the pub was packed, and all the sound went off and when I looked over the mains plug was out by the wall. So I went over to the bloke by it and said, "What was that for mate?" He said: "I never touched it mate."

So I put the plug back in. There was gang of lads there who saw this and thought they'd have some fun with it and they were planning to pull it out so I would say something and then probably get flattened.

So I sat there, and said a little prayer asking for help, and just after I said it, in through the pub door came Monk Wallace, and he sat down right over the plug, so they couldn't get at it. So the lads lost interest and they disappeared. And Monk said: "Hello Charl it's good to see you." And I said: "It's marvellous to see you Monk, you'll never know how good it is to see you." Somebody up there was definitely looking after me that night.

It's funny how what you say or do can have an impact without you knowing it. At that time I was very fervent and I used to have a little Jesus sticker on my guitar. I even had a Jesus sticker on the back of my little van. Once I pulled up outside a pub in the Ford and this fella came out and was helping me to carry stuff in. As we came out again I said: "I don't usually see you in here." I forget his name.

He said: "No I don't usually come here. I'm seeing a bird here." Now, he was married.

I said: "I'm very disappointed in you." And I pointed to the little sticker on my van and said: "You should take more notice of what this man says. But it's your life."

I went in and played and all night he sat looking at me, not in a nasty way, he was a nice bloke really. But months later I met him and he said: "You were right you know what you said that night. I packed that in that night, and I'm treading the right road now."

Now some people might have said it was presumptuous of me to have said anything to him but I never said it in a bad way and I think God uses us all in different ways. I didn't mean to pontificate in any way. I was just disappointed in him because I liked him, you know.

There was a pastor called Jimmy who used to be a right wheeler-dealer. He used to get old cars and flog them off. He said to me one day his lad was sick, and was in a bad way in the front room, when these two blokes knocked on his door. They were ministers and he said: "I'm not interested, my lad's ill."

They offered to help but again he said no, but they said: "Surely letting us in won't do any harm?" So he gave in and he let them in and they prayed for him. And his lad got better – dramatically so.

Jimmy became a minister. He was quite a charismatic chap – I don't know where he is now – but I remember him coming to our house after our Charlie had been hit in the face playing cricket and he had a bump on his face.

Jimmy prayed over him and you could see this bump fading and something definitely happened to Charlie – the whole demeanor on his face was affected. It was quite powerful actually. I think Charlie became almost as fervent as me. As I say, I don't know where Jimmy is now.

But Charlie became known as a little preacher at the school, and it caused a bit of trouble for Jamie because he fought a lot, especially at secondary school, because of the way Charlie was.

Charlie once believed that God had told him to give a message out to the whole school. He went to the teacher to ask if he could say something at assembly and the teacher said no. Anyway he was convinced that he needed to say something so in the middle of Assembly from the floor of the hall he shouted his message out.

Everybody was silent. And they called me up to the school and said that they were very worried about him and they thought he was a bit round the bend or whatever.

Now I knew he was a bit dramatic and he could be a bit of an actor so I asked: "How did he look when he did it?" And the teacher said that, in fairness, he had looked white and he was shaking, he obviously wasn't happy doing it.

I said: "I'm very proud of him to have done something that he felt was right in the face of what could have been a lot of ridicule, I think that was very courageous and I'm delighted with him." And that was that.

I don't know what they thought of me. In fact, another time, the same school called me up and said that Jamie was stealing. This time I said: "If you'd said he was being mischievous or whatever I'd have accepted it but my son is not a thief." They said: "Well this girl said she saw him doing it."

About a week later the girl went and told the teacher that it wasn't Jamie at all, it was this other lad. So I was redeemed. And our Jamie was absolutely delighted that I had spoken up and defended him.

But, you see, I knew him.

# 15. Humble Beginnings

NOW that I've been thinking back to how it all got started, little flashbacks come to mind, like how I first used to play in the bathroom, or the landing, because it sounded good to me there.
But I was that shy that if anybody came in I would stop immediately.

And how I got in with my first band – I think it was my cousin Jimmy who heard some lads were looking for a guitarist.

I didn't even have my own guitar at that time, so it was one of theirs that I played. It was lead guitar that I was playing, which tells you how primitive the group was – but I wasn't bad at that time.

They were called The Top Spots and they came from Lloyd's Corner in Wallasey which seemed a long way to me – it's actually only a couple of miles away. We had very little equipment – one snare drum with a lad sat behind it, home made amplifiers.

The first gig we did was the Bird In Hand in Wallasey, and the Naval Club on the banks of the river Mersey.

I think our payment for the night was two pints of bitter each. I was very shy and I used to sit behind the band – they were all strutting their stuff – playing the guitar. Humble beginnings.

They came to see me one day – I'd let them down a few times with them being so far away as I saw it – and I wasn't in but they left a message to say: "Tell Charlie not to let us down on this next gig because we're playing the Grosvenor Ballroom with the Silver Beatles," which is what the Fab Four were called then. I didn't turn up and I still regret that because I would have met the lads in their formative years when they were really starting to do something.

So that was one of my major regrets, musically.

I then left that band and years later I was working in the fibre glass factory. I met a lad called Pete Cook from Lloyd's Corner, and I told him that I used to play with The Top Spots, and he doubted me at first and then said: "Oh yeah, you're Charlie aren't you?"

And he told me that the band went on to become The Undertakers who went on to be a leading light in the Mersey Beat scene.

I missed a big boat there when the Mersey Beat scene took off – I was in the army in Germany and missed the whole thing.

The other major missed opportunity occurred when Ron Thomas, who I'd been with in the bands in Germany, contacted me and asked me to go down to meet him in Worthing, where he lived: "We'll go together to London because Roy Orbison's opening a studio."

Now there was a connection here because Ron's brother-in-law was a great mechanic, and Roy Orbison was a car fanatic, and whenever he came to England he would seek a particular model, and this fellow would find one and do whatever repairs might be necessary, and it would be shipped out to Roy Orbison's car museum. He would invite this lad to his show whenever he was over, so there was a good link there.

Roy Orbison said he was opening the studio, and the lad asked if Ron could come down and audition, and Roy agreed. So Ron contacted me.

I borrowed the money off Arthur for my train fare down there, and when I arrived in Worthing I was greeted by Ron Thomas who told me that Roy's family had died in a fire, and he'd obviously gone straight back home.

It was a major tragedy for him, and a very minor one for me, with me stranded on the south coast having to make my way back home.

My cousin, Jimmy Triggs, who was responsible for getting me

into The Top Spots also played a little bit himself, and he had all sorts of gear including electric guitars that he couldn't play particularly.

He seemed to spend most of his time at gigs trying to get the stuff to work. But he asked me to come and play with his band – The Atomics – in a club in the Dingle in Liverpool.

Jimmy was on the electric guitar, playing not very well, the bass player was about six foot seven, standing with one foot on a stool, and the drummer was about sixty – they were all getting on a bit and there was very little movement out of any of them.

I was on acoustic guitar and was that embarrassed, I was trying to hide behind a side curtain. Then Stanley, Jimmy's brother, said: "Give the guitar to Charlie" – at least I could play some of the old Chuck Berry stuff, so after the break I got the electric guitar and redeemed it slightly.

But I think The Atomics exploded before they got there.

The real break for me came in January 1995. The previous autumn, Foster and Allen had asked me to support them on their 1995 Spring Tour.

So I thought, I'll take a chance, I had no money really but I was ready to pack teaching in, and I thought I'd be playing to people who already like my stuff.

But I then got a phone call from Tony that January to say they were sorry but they weren't having a support now.

And I put the phone down, feeling a bit down to say the least, and I thought, maybe I should give this up. I'm fifty years of age and everywhere I turn I get nowhere, and I was feeling a bit sorry for myself.

But then the next morning I thought, no, I'm not giving up, I think this is the only thing I can do, so instead of moping around I'll think of something positive.

There was a show on RTE with Pat Kenny called Kenny Live,

which I'd been on once before although there had been no follow–
up album, so I phoned the show and asked tentatively if they'd be
interested in having me on.

And they said that they'd been trying to get me for a month, could
I get over there that week?

I don't think I could go that week because I had a cold, but I went
the following week, and I had a wonderful time.

Pat asked me to do a song, so I did *Forever Friend*, and then Pat
asked that if there was time at the end of the show would I come
back and do another one.

At the end of the show I was hanging around the wings in case he
called me back. He was talking to a chap in the audience who
stuttered really badly, and was taking a long time to respond to Pat's
questions.

I thought that I had blown my chance, because he wouldn't have
time to bring me back on. I was all set to head back to the dressing
room, but they even extended the show, I think, to let me finish the
song – I did *What Colour is the Wind* with just my acoustic guitar
and bass pedals.

I had a large captive audience that night because the Irish Lottery
followed the show so the whole of Ireland was watching.

I had a great weekend in Dublin, and the following week my son
Jamie was picking me up from school, and he said: "Hey Dad,
you're in the Irish charts."

I said: "What am I 98?" I would have been delighted with
anything you know. He said: "No Dad, you're Number Two."

And the following week I was Number One – I'd knocked off
Garth Brooks, who was really big in Ireland at that time, and Celine
Dion – there were all sorts of people in that chart.

When they sent me a copy of the chart a while after, it looked like
the world was playing a joke on me, because all these big names
where on there – Simple Minds, The Chieftains, even Elvis was

there – and on the top of this list was my name and it didn't look real, it didn't look right you know? But it was and I was delighted.

So I'd got that opening for myself, and when I got that break, it was because all of Ireland had watched the show and then gone in the shops clamouring for me, which was great to hear.

Thankfully at the time I had this album out with Ritz Records and they were in place to feed the demand.

So that's what put me at the top of the charts, and it was amazing because even up to a year afterwards I was still in that chart.

The whole world exploded for me then, because Ritz said to pack my job in, and I was a little bit worried although I wanted to do it, I wanted to know if my family would be alright.

Mick Clerkin, the boss of Ritz, who's a good friend of mine, said: "Charlie you'll have nothing to worry about on that score, you'll be fine."

So I worked another six days after that – the staff were all delighted for me and I left.

Terry Bradford had produced the album in Birmingham with a group of musicians from that area, and when the record broke, Ritz told Terry to get a band together ready to go on the road, so he quickly got the band together from those lads.

We had Terry on guitar and his wife Suzy as backing singer, and Pete Ariss on bass, Paul on drums, Bob Willis on keyboards and Pete Ware who'd help produce the album, so all these people knew all the stuff.

We went to rehearse in Birmingham and Terry was quite a hard taskmaster.

When we went on the road, the one who found it the hardest was me – I didn't really know my own songs, although I'd written them, I hadn't that much cause to sing most of them.

I think you really learn a song when you've sung it a few times, so lyrics weren't really etched into my memory at all. So, it was a bit nerve racking for me, plus I had to remember the discipline of playing with a band, whereas I'd been used to singing things on my own where I could stretch timing out and change things.

If you're singing in a band you have to stick to the format of any particular song, so it was a little bit difficult for me.

We went on the road in Ireland and the first gig was in Ballymena, up in the north in the Town Hall.

In fact I've just recently come back from a tour in Ireland, and they've done that same place up as a beautiful arts centre.

But that's where we started, and it was a great relief that it went down as well as it did.

We all met up the night before the show – some new faces included Tony Maguire, who I'd never met before and who was looking after me, and Pat Nolan who controlled all the sound and lighting guys – and we had a few pints and got to know each other, and had a great laugh.

The next night after that was Dublin's Gaiety Theatre – this was big stuff to me because I'd come from playing little dockside pubs and suddenly I'm in front of big crowds.

They were all sold out because I was at the top of the charts, and their expectations were a bit of a burden for me to bear.

In those days I used to be sat out in the front, and there was a big gap between me and the band – none of my doing – so you felt it was you alone against the world.

And it was particularly nerve-racking because everyone was there – Daniel O'Donnell came to that one – and there were TV and press people about, but thankfully it went down great.

I came off stage shaking like a leaf, with a mix of euphoria and relief that it had gone well. Ireland's always been good to me but that first run was more than a bit nerve-racking. And in all honesty, I think I floated along on a sea of alcohol.

I'm not an alcoholic, or blind drunk, but I'm not the most

confident person in the world and it was a bit daunting, plus I was doing all sorts of interviews left right and centre, so it was quite stressful.

Everywhere you went people knew you, which was lovely but it was a bit stressful and a very strenuous time, as enjoyable as it was.

We then produced other albums – With You In Mind and Further Down The Road – and we'd go on tour every spring and autumn, which we continue to do now.

# 16. Ireland: Land of the Quiet Man

WHEN I first started writing songs, although I'd never been to Ireland, I'd always liked the idea of Ireland.

I liked every Irish person I'd ever met and I liked the way they talked and the sense of humour, and I suppose some of it was an idealistic vision of Ireland you get from watching films like The Quiet Man.

When I did eventually get to go – I was invited by Tony Allen of Foster and Allen to go to his home in Moate, in County West Meath – I must admit that when I was leaving I had mixed feelings.

I was a little bit apprehensive – an Englishman going into Ireland and I thought I might be met with some hostility. I think I'd only been there a day when I realised how stupid that was. At that time nobody had ever heard of me and I was always treated with nothing but kindness.

Once I settled in I loved the place – with good reason – everyone loved the music and it was fun and I thought I'd gone to a sort of larger Merseyside because the same sort of attitude to life prevailed there.

I went into the Palace Bar in Athlone with Tony Allen, and when we walked in the whole place was buzzing with: "Tony Allen's there," and "Look, Tony Allen's in," and Seamus Shannon, who's a marvellous accordion player and a great character – singer-song writer and a funny man as well – said: "Ah, two famous people have just walked into the bar – our own Tony Allen and a great singer-songwriter from Liverpool, Charlie Landsborough."

And of course they're all saying: "Charlie who? Never heard of him." Anyway I sat down next to this fella and he said: "Is that right now, Charlie, you write the songs? What did you write?"

I said: "Well, Tony's recorded some of them, I wrote *Part Of Me.*"

I mentioned some others but he looked completely blank and said: "To be sure, I've never heard of them."

I said: "It doesn't matter. I'm not at all offended." And we had a bit of a laugh together and a couple of pints. He got up to go and as he got to the door he turned around and he said: "God bless you Charlie Landsborough. I enjoyed your company very much. Have a marvellous holiday in Ireland, and next time you write a song will you write a bloody song I've heard of?"

I thought this is great, it's like Spike Milligan Land this. I went to the bar the same night and there were two old characters at the bar.

One of them said: "Where do you come from Charlie?" I said "Birkenhead near Liverpool." And they weren't acting the goat, they were straight-faced and everything – one turned to the other and said: "To be sure if he never opened his mouth I'd never know where he come from." I sat down somewhat bemused, but I felt as though I'd gone to a second home.

Moate is only a little village and it's not the most picturesque, it's flat in the middle of Ireland and there's just this one big wide main street with about seventeen pubs in it, but there's some great characters there, especially then on that first trip.

I was naive enough in those days to believe that Irish pubs closed at closing time. The lads would invite me for a session – a session in the pub. And I'd park my car, and go in somewhere for a coffee and when I came out there would be a little note behind the wipers saying 'See you tonight.'

I'd go in there at about eight o' clock, thinking they'd all be in there, and they'd turn up at quarter to ten, and it would go on from there, for ages and ages, playing and laughing and singing – it was unbelievable.

I remember the Garda coming once and throwing us all out, but you were allowed to take your drink with you. So I'm standing on the pavement with lots of other people and I've got a pint of Guinness in one hand and my guitar in the other, and as soon as he disappeared the Boss said: "Alright lads back in now." And we're all back in again. So it was a lovely place.

There were some great characters there – 'Bless My Soul' he was a real old gentleman and Thelma used to say that he looked like he'd got ready thirty years ago and never changed since.

He looked a little bit shoddy but he was a lovely old character. He used to sit bolt upright – he couldn't half knock his drink back – and I remember them all talking one night about people who had inherited farms and who had drunk it all away and Oliver said: "One farm? I drank two!" So he drank two farms, but he used to pray for me every night. I don't think he had very much in the end although he'd lived quite a high life in his early days.

When I would leave the town I would present them with a bottle of whisky – there was a pub called The Elbow ran by a friend of mine called Pat Claffey – a marvellous man and a great pub manager, and I would leave the bottle of whisky with him to dole out to Bless My Soul and Paddy, who liked his whisky.

Now it says something for a pub manager who would share out a bottle of whisky and make nothing from it. He told them that Charlie had left a bottle of whisky for them and they'd call in each day to have "one of Charlie's" and he'd give them a tot of the whisky. Of course with them both nipping in, it didn't last very long, and when it had gone they practically accused Pat of helping himself to it. And he was doing them a favour letting them have it for nothing.

But I loved those characters in that town.

They called him Bless My Soul because he'd say: "God Bless My Soul it's the hairy gentleman," and that was me of course. He was lovely. I remember an Irish television crew making a documentary and asking me where I would like it to be and I said Moate and they were amazed that I picked this little town, but the people in it were great and the atmosphere was great. And at one point they came to the pub and I was talking to Oliver, which was Bless My Soul's real name and I said: "It's lovely to see you, how are you?" "Oh I'm fine," he says.

We talked some more and I said: "Well I'm very disappointed Oliver because you haven't said my favourite expression yet." He said: "Bless my soul what's that?"

He was great, he lived in a tiny place just on the edge of town, and he had really old furniture, and one day we were passing and there was an old cast iron bedstead at the start of the main road with a 'For Sale' sign on it, so I think he was supplementing what little income he had with selling bits of his furniture off from time to time.

And then there was little Willie, who was a fine accordion player. He had this little mischievous smile about him, and I think when I first met him the lads had been telling him about me, and he didn't know what to expect of me.

I met him in the pub and he came out with a slightly sarcastic comment so I just smiled and said something similar back. He had this big smile on his face and we were the best of friends from there on in. I loved hearing him play his accordion.

Now, the kerb in Moate is very high, and Willy was coming out of The Elbow and fell down and I think he broke his leg, and finished up in hospital. So I went to see him and I asked him how he was and he said: "I'm grand. I may be over to see you in the autumn. I'll have a few bob – I've put a claim in and I'm expecting a big payout."

But he told them, when he made his claim, that he had been

coming out of the butchers. So after a while I asked Pat Claffy: "What happened to Willy, did he get anything?"

To which Pat replied: "He nearly got nine months." Apparently when it got to court they asked him again where he was coming from when he fell and again he said it was the butchers. So the court then wanted to know why it took them 24 hours to dry him out before they could do anything for him. He'd been full of drink you see. And the lads used to pull his leg silly after that when he came in The Elbow: "Would you like a drink Willy, or would you prefer a leg of lamb or a fillet steak?" He was a funny character.

When we stayed with Tony Allen we never expected him to take us anywhere, we just used to get in the car and take ourselves off. If he wanted to take us somewhere we'd go but he would never feel under any duress to look after us.

We'd drive off, and we'd be here there and everywhere, and we'd just phone him when we got there. This particular night we'd ended up in County Clare and it was getting late. We thought we'd better be getting back to West Meath, but we saw this pub and thought we'd have a quick drink first. To be honest it looked a bit miserable, this place, but I went into the bar. I thought it was near closing time, but I managed to get a drink for myself and Thelma, and thought I'd ask what time they closed. I had, by now, heard all the answers like "October," but I asked the manager anyway. He just gave a little mischievous smile and said: "Say nothing and drink your drink."

So I thought: "That's a good sign." And these three lads kicked off playing music. There weren't many other people in there. So I asked if I could join them, went and got my guitar out of the car, and started playing with them. Then I played a few on my own, and the manager was bringing out sausages and toast and drinks and it was great. I think I came out of there at about four in the morning.

I had to sleep in the car because I couldn't drive – I'd had too much too drink. They were saying to me: "Who are you?" and I often wonder if, later when I was on the telly, they saw me and thought, "Ah that's who he was." We never did make it back to West Meath that night.

When I went back to Moate, once I'd made my name and they were doing the documentary on me, I wanted it to be set in The Elbow, because it was an old pub and it had a potbelly stove in the corner, it was pretty primitive but I liked it – it had atmosphere and it had the characters. It's all changed now, and I don't like it. But when we turned up there the bar was closed for refurbishment so we had to bring in the pint of Guinness from next door and pretend the bar was working. But we had a great time.

One night Pat, Willy, myself and some others, including Josey Adamson who played the box as well, decided to go across the border to County Offaly to The Cat and Bagpipes. Moate was only just over the border of Meath and Offaly, so you could walk to this pub.

It was one of those lovely old quaint Irish pubs that was also a little grocer's store. As you walked in, there was a little room with a grocery area, and two older brothers ran the place. When you passed through the grocery area, there was a door to the little bar – small and primitive but a proper bar – and I took my guitar in and the others brought their stuff in, and were looked at with a bit of suspicion to begin with.

But then they warmed to us and they were very nice. I think I sat on a beer crate – there weren't many seats and what there were weren't up to much – and we played and had a lovely night, and then tootled off. The following week Pat said to me that he'd met the manager of The Cat and Bagpipes and he had said to Pat: "D'you know who we had in the pub the other week? You'll never believe it. It was that long grey-haired fella Charlie Landsberry, and d'you know that if we'd not have known who he was we'd never have let him in."

And I thought the cheeky devil. It looked like it had been furnished from Bosnia and they weren't going to let me in because I didn't fit the bill. But they were very nice to me.

Pat told me that apparently when times were hard – it was only a little village and they didn't have much – when the villagers were struggling to afford food, they were giving away food from the pub, and looking after people. They were really lovely people. So that was The Cat and Bagpipes.

I was in a bar once with Thelma and our Jamie, and I could see Tony and Josey stood at the bar laughing. So I went over to ask what they were laughing at. Now there's a bit of a character in the town called Red McCann – a bit of a wide-boy but very likeable and he plays what he called The Skittle, which is a long sort of pole with nails knocked into it with loads of bottle tops on and little notches cut out of it – he's amazing to watch with a fantastic sense of rhythm.

He dances with it and taps it and you'd have to see him to believe it. So Tony tells me this story about a local farmer whose gate went missing and Red went to see him and asked if he wanted a gate for his field. Red said he could get one for 15 pounds. The farmer agreed and the next day Red went around with the gate and the farmer was delighted and gave him his money.

But later, when Red had gone, the farmer was going around his field and another gate was missing. Red had sold him his own gate.

So Tony's telling me this and I'm laughing heartily and then Tony asks Josey if the farmer had said anything to Red. "No. And it's just as well," says Josey "Because he might have taken a fence." I know it's corny but it's good isn't it?

There was another character in Moate, an Englishman called John Isherwood. Apparently he'd gone on holiday to Moate and just never went home. I think one of his brothers was a bishop, and another was an architect, so he was from a very good family, and I think his own sons were very clever. But John went to Moate and just dropped out and got by doing a bit of sign writing. He had once been a recording artist with Decca, writing his own stuff. He had a bit of a weakness for the old drink – he'd do a letter, then he'd ask for a bit of a payment to get a drink, then do another letter, and it went on like that. And he let himself go a bit.

In fact I wrote the song *The Bluebell Man* for him because he was writing a book at the time called The Bluebell Man. He wasn't eating very well, in fact they found him dead a few years back – which I found very sad because I really liked John.

Anyway, we were in Pat's little terraced house one night having a session, and John was there looking a bit worse for wear, so Pat's wife took him upstairs to shampoo his hair. And when he came down and sat with a drink in his hand while she blew his hair dry, he looked fantastic. He had this long beautiful hair.

He was sat in the pub the next day and we'd never seen him looking so well – his hair was gleaming and he had good clothes on, he looked great. But what I couldn't get over, was come the next day it looked as though it had never happened. He looked as dishevelled as ever he had done. But for that brief moment we had seen John in all his glory and it was wonderful.

John was writing this book and said: "Charlie I'm writing a book called The Bluebell Man. Would you write a song for it?"

Now I had my own idea of who the Bluebell Man would be – a sort of cross between the pied piper and St Francis of Asissi – a sort of mystical figure. So I wrote this song which hopefully is along those lines.

And then he told me what this book was about. It was like something Spike Milligan would have written. He told me about this one section where there was this farmer who had discovered that if you put wires in a potato you can gel an electrical charge from it. He decided that instead of buying a new battery for his hearing aid, he'd string a load of potatoes on wire like a belt around him. So he did and he blew his head off – that's how ridiculous the book was – and I'd written this sort of ethereal song for it.

I don't think he ever finished the book. But he was great to talk to – he had memories of Spike Milligan, and Peter Sellers and Peter Cook who he'd met. He'd even got a cheque from George Harrison for some comedy thing he'd written, which I told him would be worth something as a collector's item. But it was sad to see him go downhill – our Jamie loved him.

I've never seen a sadder looking sight than when we were driving through Moate on the one day of the year when all the pubs were closed. There was Paddy sat on the side of the road staring at the pub that was closed. I'd loved to have captured that expression – the pained yearning and helplessness – with a camera. It was marvellous to see.

In the same village we had a little session, with Pat Claffey on the snare drum, Josey on squeeze box and me on the guitar. One of the lads there invited us back to his house, which was a big old place, but, he said, we had to be quiet because his mother slept at the back of the house. As we were crossing the step, trying to be quiet, Pat (who was the most sensible of all of us) dropped the snare drum and it rolled all through the house. But we never woke the lad's mother up. And we had such a great time that we all ended up, Thelma included, sleeping in different rooms.

In the morning I woke up and I had to go to the toilet and I felt terrible because the poor lady wouldn't have known we were there.

But when I got up I saw her in the kitchen, and she was cooking a load of food. So I apologised to her but she said: "Not at all. Now when you're done come in here and help yourself to whatever you want. A big man like you needs his food."

And the last thing I felt like was some food but she was nice as pie and typical of most of the Irish people I met.

# 17. A Home From Home

IT'S lovely, as a singer, to see that what you do has an effect on someone.

I was singing that lovely old Irish song *Come Home Paddy Riley* to Bally James Duff, and there was a great big hulk of a man standing at the bar crying. I think it was for the right reasons – I think he was touched by the music – and you sort of wonder whether you are doing the right thing. But it was nice to see because obviously it had affected him.

Around the same time, they asked me if I'd play in the Palace, Athlone. It was in the upstairs room, and was run by Paddy – another lovely fella. All the crowd from Moate, which was five miles up the road, came by bus.

We had a great time and afterwards I sat with Paddy talking for a while. We still got back to Moate before they all did because that little bus they were on kept stopping for each of them to give a song or a story. So they got home a long time after us. They were great supporters and still are.

My trips to Moate were usually in school holidays and sometimes at Christmas. But I was invariably late, because on the day I'd be due to go back, someone would say "Your boat's been cancelled."

And I'd have to stay and then make up excuses as to why I was late. Sometimes they were genuine and sometimes they weren't. Sometimes we were snowed in, or Thelma got food poisoning, but they were used to me. In fact I've still got a note from the deputy headmaster, John Owen – they used to send notes around the staff – and this one said: "A special note for Charlie. School begins on January 7th."

And when I'd come back late you could see him not believing a word that I was saying, but smiling to himself. In fact one time, I arrived back from Ireland on time and on the Sunday night I phoned up the Head – Mr Fallows - and said in a heavy Irish accent: "Hello is that Mr Bellows?" He said "Mr Fallows." I said "That's right Mr Bellows, I've got some very bad news for you about Charlie Landsborough. He will be in school tomorrow." And then he laughed.

When we went to Tony Allen's home, with Thelma and Jamie, who was only a little lad then, I was worrying as to whether Tony's wife Maureen would mind us all descending on her because I'd never met her.

But I think we'd been there five minutes and I was thinking she was lovely – like a sister to me and Thelma, so that was that worry out of the way. I remember I used to do a few little tricks that Cliffy Starkey had shown me, and I was showing them to Tony's little lads and Keith said to me "Will you show me the trick Charlie?"

I said: "I can't because I was given the secret by the Grand Wizard in England, and I'm sworn to secrecy and I can't tell you how to do it."

He was sat on my knee and stroking my beard and he said in a little crafty Irish way: "Ah Charlie, tell me. The Wizard will never see you over here in Ireland."

But I didn't show him, I kept the mystique.

I was in Pat Claffey's house one day and he'd been down with his sons cutting the peat. I asked him what his sons got for helping with that. "A warm arse," replied Paddy. I was expecting him to say a couple of bob or something. And that was his answer, to the point, but not so sensitively put. He told me a story of an American and his wife who stopped a man on the road and asked the way to Galway.

He told them, and off they went to Galway. On their way back they stopped at a pub for drink, and as they went in they saw the same old man sitting in a corner.

The wife says to her husband to go and buy him a drink for giving them the directions to Galway. So he goes over to him and buys him a drink. And then another and another, and eventually the American says to him: "I think I've been sent here today by God. And I come to show you the way to God"

The little old Irish fellow says to him: "Show me the way to God?

"You didn't know the way to Galway this morning."

I don't know if that story's true or not but I like to believe it is.

When I recorded Songs From The Heart in Tony Allen's studio in Moate it was produced by Desi Hines who's partially sighted.

He used to play in Tony's band and he was a keyboard player and a fine penny whistle player, and he does a really good Irish dance as well. We thought we should pay him a visit, on one of our trips over there, and he finished up taking us to the pub. He took his accordion with him and I borrowed an old guitar off them from behind the bar, and we kicked off.

We were only supposed to be going for a cup of tea but we left there two days later. But you can't call on an Irish family and expect to get away with just a cup of tea.

During that recording I was singing *Walking On My Memories* and I was singing this particular line and the lad behind the desk said: "What are you singing Charlie?"

I said: "Past the house he knew." "It doesn't sound like it," he said as he was laughing. I kept going over it contorting my face, trying to articulate it and they were getting more tickled by the minute and in the end I had a brain wave and said: "Right I've got it now."

And I sang: "By the house he knew," and they laughed and said

"Well he's re-writing his songs now to accommodate his Scouse accent."

Tony said he'd take us to a real old Irish pub. He took us down this lane, and pulled up outside this ordinary house. We went in through the front door and in the front room there were men and women stood all around the walls.

There was a fella playing a squeezebox, a young lad playing a bass (powered I think by a car battery) and there was a little passageway with a cloakroom with older fellas sitting there. We went into the back room and I went up to order a drink for us.

Amongst other things, I asked for a whisky and water and said: "Would you put some water in the whisky with the water in it," or something stupid like that, and I said: "God bless us I've only been here a week and I'm talking like you."

He said: "If you're here another week we may start understanding you."

I don't think that place will still be there but that was an insight into old Ireland, if you like.

When I was going to Moate I wrote a song, about Ireland really, because it sort of paints a very romantic vision.

I used to play it to old Olly, who had a permanent little smile but tinged with sadness, with these Labrador's eyes like, and they used to well up when I played it. Sadly he's not here any more either but it was those great characters that I went there for.

Pat Claffey went up to the north and came back with about seven pairs of glasses. I asked him: "What's all the glasses for, Pat? You don't wear glasses." He said: "I know, but in The Elbow there was only one fella who had glasses, and they were passing them around when they were picking their horses out."

So he'd bought all these glasses back to leave behind the bar. I thought that was hilarious.

When I was playing in the pubs around Moate, Pat really liked what I did and he believed in me. And I was sitting talking to him one day and I said: "D'you know Pat, if I was ever to get a break I'd love it to be in Ireland. I know it's not the biggest market in the world but I just love the place." And that's exactly what happened, when I did get my break, so the Lord answered my request.

When Foster and Allen recorded *I Will Love You All My Life* most people didn't know I'd written it, even in my own town. I was playing in a little pub in Anglesey and this blind lady came in, who was a bit loud and obnoxious.

I was singing *I Will Love You All My Life* and she shouts out "You want to learn the words to that song." And the bloke who was sitting next to her, who knew me, leaned over and said: "I'd be quiet if I were you love, he actually wrote the song."

So she was telling me to learn the words to my own song. Needless to say she was somewhat embarrassed and left, which everybody was pleased about.

Now before Bless My Soul died, his relatives wanted to send him across to Manchester to see other relatives he hadn't seen in donkey's years. And they said to him: "Now Oliver, somebody's going to take you to Dublin airport and you'll fly to Manchester, you'll be met at the airport and taken to see the family." To which he replied: "You'll not get me up in one of them things." And they said: "Oh Oliver, when your number's up it's up." So he says: "What if it's the driver's number that's up?"

Years later when I did get the break, we were touring Ireland and I was playing Sligo and this request came through to say would I attend the commemoration of the famine, in Tuam Cathedral.

This was a great honour really because I was the only English man there. The Taoiseach was there, and other dignitaries from all the various churches, and other performers were there – all Irish – and me. I sang *Forever Friends*, just on acoustic guitar, to the combined gathered dignitaries and I had a smashing time. And afterwards they laid on a bit of a meal for us and this gentleman came over to me, who I'd never seen in my life, and he stuck this thing in my hand and said: "Thanks Charlie," and walked off.

I thought it would be a religious medal or something but when I opened my hand it was an actual coin from 1852, with the Queen's head on and I thought, what a wonderful gesture, to give this to somebody you didn't know.

I've still got it to this day. I was so taken with this, that when I played in Galway I managed to contact him through the radio station and I invited him to the show as a gesture of thanks for the wonderful thing he had done for me.

Anyway, that night after the show they took me to a local pub where there was an All Ireland match on, I think. Eventually when I got back to the hotel – I was much later than I expected to be – and I went to my room, but there was no Thelma. So I went to the desk and asked did they know what had happened to Mrs Landsborough, and they said she'd left. I thought oh no . . . So I asked if she said where she was going and they said no.

I thought, oh I know, she'll be going to Tony Allen's just outside of Moate. I phoned through to the police station in a little village that I knew was on the way, and I said: "There's a taxi coming through with my wife in it, could you stop it and tell her that I'm here and could she come back and we'll sort it out?"

She wasn't well pleased. And that couldn't happen in England, but the Garda did stop her and you can imagine what she told me to do through them, and she carried on, which must have caused them some hilarity. So I had to follow on and you can imagine the cost of the taxi, if you know Ireland – it's a fair old distance – you'll know it cost a small fortune. But we patched it up.

It was a real honour though to be a non-Irish performer commemorating the Famine, which had terrible repercussions for the people of Ireland at that time.

# 18. The Turning of the Tide

NOT many people read autobiographies all the way through – some dipping in and dipping out.

So I thought I'd have one chapter where I tie up all lose ends. If I didn't call this book *Storyteller* it would be *That's The Way The Wind Blows*.

Music is pivotal in my life and I think that without key people certain situations and a lot of luck – both good AND bad – I wouldn't be where I am today.

Now in what I call a little documentary in print, this is the story of Charlie Landsborough musician, and how I got here.

After this section, stay with 'the show' and the rest of my book and enjoy getting to know me a bit better.

So . . . I got a listening audience in country music clubs and started taking bookings from two people who believed in me – Neil Coppendale used to book me for his festival and then started booking me for some clubs down in the south of England and, later, Frank Campbell from Buxton gave me some bookings.

But these gigs often involved me travelling long distances, often way down south, in places like Norfolk and getting home very late in the morning and not getting a lot of money for it.

Me and Thelma often slept in our car which we called the Volvo Hotel. I once did a tour with Mary Duff and that's where we slept every night. Early on we never even had sleeping bags. But at least

I was doing what I loved, and meeting nice people and enjoying myself, but not seeming to make any huge strides towards success.

By this time I had written a number of songs because I thought that might be the key that would unlock the door to success – I thought I was getting nowhere singing other people's stuff so I started writing my own songs.

I began to have some success with Foster and Allen and George Hamilton IV and I sent a little demo off. It was heard by Ralph Norton, from down south, who managed Little Ginny, a country singer on the British scene who had recorded my song *No Time At All*. Ralph got in touch with me and asked if I had any more stuff.

So I sent him a lot of songs off and he told me that he was very impressed. He signed me as a songwriter and then he suggested that I go into the studio and record a couple of songs.

I recorded *I Will Love You All My Life* – it was a very small affair but nonetheless it did trigger a huge response. I remember at the time that Ed Stewart played it as his record of the week on Radio Two, which was astonishing because it was no big record label or anything like that, and people in Ireland were turned on to this and couldn't get hold of it.

I remember hearing that Foster and Allen heard the song while travelling through England and liked it.

Then when they got to London, Bill Delaney, who was involved with them, said: "I've got a great song for you," and he played this track, and Foster and Allen told him they'd heard it and liked it but felt it had already been done.

But Bill knew that it was hard to get hold of it – it had had no great distribution deal behind it, so they recorded it and had a hit with it and got into our hit parade, I think, and had a big success in South Africa and Australia with that song. And that's how my relationship with Foster and Allen came about, as a songwriter.

But I didn't seem to be getting any further. Then my friendship developed with Tony Allen and he encouraged me to record an album in his studio.

So I recorded Songs From My Heart and I was delighted to have had something at last recorded by myself. It didn't make huge inroads, but Gerry Anderson, up in the north of Ireland, a wonderful presenter and DJ – and now a great friend of mine – started playing this and he got a great reaction.

I was asked to do interviews with Gerry and I remember I rode home from the school on my bike to do this interview, in my break.

And after I'd finished and rode back to school, people were ringing him up asking him to put me on his television show called Anderson On The Box. And that was exactly what he did, and I went over to sing on his show.

Now long before this happened I'd been playing in a little club near Frodsham and this character, by the name of John Smith, came over to me and said: "You should be in Northern Ireland – they'd love you up there."

"Thanks, but I don't think I'll ever get there," I said to him.

And he started coming to see me play – initially he'd thought I was an American playing over here, but when he found out I was a local lad he began to come to the gigs, and we became really good friends. He gave a tape of mine, which I'd paid for myself, to his friend in Northern Ireland, Sean Coyle.

Now Sean hadn't been able to get it to play, but he must have remembered my name because he was a great friend of Gerry Anderson. And then of course, we get to the point where Gerry is playing my CD, and him and Sean contacted me and brought me over, with Thelma, and they brought John Smith over as my manager.

Smithy was unemployed at the time because he'd been made redundant from his job at the Coal Board. And it was strange how all this came to pass because he was the first one to say I should be in Northern Ireland, when I never thought I'd get there, and then when I do make it over there, this same John Smith travels with me as manager. We did the show and then we travelled on to do the pubs, and the journey itself was a bit of a marathon because I was playing in Norfolk, then I drove all the way back to Merseyside from Great Yarmouth, pick Smithy up on the way, go home and pick up Thelma and the tickets, then drive up to Stranraer in Scotland, and then go across on the boat to Northern Ireland.

We were sitting in the bar, and this lad kept poking his head around the corner of the bar looking at me. Next thing there was a message called out that there was someone waiting for Charlie Landsborough, and it turned out to be this lad, Martin McAllister, who was going to be playing guitar with me on the show the following day.

I'd never met him before in my life but he knew me, and we went to the studios and met a lovely man called David Donaghie, who asked if we wanted to stay in a hotel or stay with him in his house.

As we liked him we stayed with him. So we got to his house and he suggested we have a run through so we played *What Colour Is The Wind* and when we finished he just said "Crap."

But I just smiled and then he smiled and said: "Ah you can only say that to a Scouser."

We got on great and had a great time on the show. Gerry had asked me, after the show, to play the pubs in Derry, which I agreed to as they were the ones who started the whole ball rolling for me so I owed it to them. So we all drove off to Derry. The first pub we played was in the heart of the Bogside, and the troubles were on at the time, and I'm no hero and felt a little bit apprehensive at the time, but they were marvellous to me.

All I would hear, when I was going into the pubs or club, would be either: "It's Derry tonight Charlie," or "It's Londonderry tonight," so you knew which side of the divide you were playing to.

But I just shut up and sang. And they couldn't have been better to me. I had a lovely family called the MacDaid's looking after me, and I played the pubs with my little bit of gear and I had a fantastic time. Smithy was great because he was back in his home town, and when we were in Belfast doing the telly they put us all up in a fantastic hotel just outside Belfast called The Culloden, one of the best hotels in the British Isles.

Now we'd never stayed anywhere like that and we were a bit hard up and Smithy couldn't get over the size of the room, or the fruit placed in it, or the trouser press which he put his tee shirt in, so we were all very impressed with the place generally.

And the following morning, as we didn't have much money, we ordered tea and toast for three, and they brought this silver salver out with the toast and butter separate. Smithy turned to me and said: "I'm very disappointed, have I got to butter this myself?"

We had a great laugh and a fantastic time.

So it happened that when I did the TV show, Pat Kenny was watching, and he liked what he saw. I was contacted and asked to go on his show, which I did. I sang *What Colour Is The Wind*, although I didn't have an album at the time with that song on it.

Pat was very gracious to me. I then left, after seeing Tony Allen for a while on the way, and that was it. Tony subsequently sold the album of mine that he'd recorded in his studio, to Ritz Records, who were a major label, especially in Irish-related music – they had Daniel O'Donnell and were very highly thought of. And Tony had passed the record on to them. But nothing much had happened and it all sort of died away a little bit.

I approached Ritz to see if they were interested in recording any more of my songs, and I think that they really wanted the songs, and not necessarily me as a fella who just sat down and sang. I didn't really fit into their working pattern, with Daniel O'Donnell and all that – I hope I'm not being unfair because Mick's a good friend of mine at Ritz, but I think that's how it was. We recorded the album in Birmingham with Terry Bradford who was an excellent producer, and he brought all these musicians in and we recorded *What Colour Is The Wind*.

It was released and nothing much happened until the January of 1995, when Tony Allen called me with the offer of a supporting tour – which subsequently didn't happen – and prompted me to make my own call to the Pat Kenny show. And that was when the ball really started rolling.

Once I'd got my break, my life changed rapidly. I was booked into a hotel in Dublin called the Burlington, and I was given a huge suite.

Now I had had only limited experience of staying in hotels, and this suite had two rooms and I kept wandering from one to the other to feel as though I was making the best of it. I remember sitting on the bed with Thelma and she suddenly said: "Remember the ha'penny?"

And she was reminding me of years ago, when my dad was sat on the back step filing a ha'penny down to go in the meter. I was going through my religious phase at the time and I told him he shouldn't be doing that, and he said: "Well Charlie, if I don't do this we haven't got any light." Years later when I was married and living in a two up and two down in Thornton Street in the North End of Birkenhead, who was sitting on the back step filing his own ha'penny?

And I thought at the time my dad would have been smiling down at me saying: "See I wasn't that bad was I son?" So to remember those times while we were being treated with such luxury was good fun.

Some funny things happen when you're on tour, and I remember staying in the Europa Hotel in Belfast which was a great hotel with smashing staff.

We'd come back after the show and we were having a few drinks in the bar, and then I went to bed. I got up in the middle of the night to go to the toilet, and I ambled towards what I thought was the toilet door, half full of drink and in a fair state of slumber, and the next thing I'm staring at a bright light, and the door clicked behind me and I realised I was a standing on the landing stark naked, not a sight to behold I can assure you, and I thought "Oh God," and I knew Thelma usually was fast asleep as soon as her head hit the pillow, so I thought I had no chance of getting back in.

I started banging on the door and I just about heard Thelma laughing – thankfully she was still awake, and she let me in. I'd had visions of half of Belfast turning up on the landing, "Come and take a look at Charlie Landsborough here and see the state of him."

Just as the success began to break, I got solo gigs in Northern Ireland, signed to Ritz and Mick Clerkin came along with me and we had a great time.

I remember going to Straban in Northern Ireland, where Charlie McBrean had booked me into the St Patrick's club. I'd never been in it before or seen it and I remember saying to Charlie, as he was busying about: "I will get a sound check won't I Charlie?"

I didn't have any on my own gear of my own at the time and was just stepping into a situation and hoping that they had a half decent sound system.

He said: "Oh yes, Charlie, everything will be fine." And I kept asking him and he kept saying the same thing. But the first time I saw the room was when I stepped out from behind the curtain in front of the audience and I said a little prayer that I might need God to help me with this one.

There was a lad looking after the system there and thankfully after the first few songs he got it together, and it was ok. But it was nerve-racking when you think of all the expectations that people have in front of you, and you're on your own.

While I was still on that same run we went to Omagh, and I was playing in a hotel there and the room where you played was around the back of the hotel, quite a way from the front. They took me around to wait by a bit of a screen that I could stand behind.

And I needed a wee, but I knew the toilet was too far away at the front of the hotel, and I didn't want to be sitting on stage and suddenly have to excuse myself to go to the toilet. Now it was very dark and there was this bin at the back of me and I thought: "That'll do, no one will see," and I started weeing into the bin.

And as I did the door suddenly opened and this voice said: "Charlie, I have Father Brian D'Arcy here to see you."

Father Brian came forward and I said: "I'm sorry about this Father," and he just laughed – he's a great character Father Brian – he was a sort of minister to the music business in Ireland.

So we had a bit of a laugh over that. Not long after they had this wonderful event in the cathedral in Enniskillen and I was asked to be the special guest. We went over and it was a huge cathedral and it was choc-a-bloc with people and they had rooms upstairs with television monitors. Father Brian Darcey invited me on to the altar where I was going to sing, and he introduced me and said to the whole of the audience: "Here's our forever friend, Charlie Landsborough, and do you know the first time that I ever met Charlie he was peeing in a bin in Omagh?"

And I said to him afterwards, "Well what a wonderful introduction that was." And he said: "Well it was the truth wasn't?" So he was a great character. That was typical Ireland, great times, great people, great fun.

I think one of the nice offshoots of success was to see the pleasure that it brought to my friends and family, who I'm sure were beginning to think, like me, that success was never going to come, and suddenly I could invite them over to these wonderful places.

I remember the first time we came back to Liverpool to play in the Philharmonic and it was a bit of a terrifying experience for me to be playing on home ground. The place was full of people I knew, who'd listened to me in the pub, or worked with me, or were family, and I said that there literally was everybody in there from safe-breakers to nuns. And it was true.

They'd all come to see what had happened to Charlie. And it went down great, although there's always more pressure on you when you're playing to home crowds, even though they're all with you.

When there was initial particular interest in me, when I'd joined Ritz, I was invited up to Aberdeen to a television show with all the Ritz artists, Daniel O Donnell, Mary Duff and others – it was like a Scotch Irish night really – and I was dreading going because I thought they wouldn't like anyone who was as old as me and couldn't dance around.

Again I had a fantastic hotel and we went to do the show and it went down great, which was a huge relief to me, because I was on my own.

And I had a marvellous weekend and they gave me an envelope full of money, so sometimes when you expect the worst it turns out best. They've been very good to me in Scotland ever since, and it proved to me that my appeal could stretch beyond Ireland, and I began to relax a bit.

I must admit that I used to calm the nerves with drink, and especially in Ireland it was easy to drink too much, and you'd be so relieved after a show that you'd drink again in the bar, and then it would get really late and you'd go to bed and before you knew it you'd have to get up again and travel to the next show.

So I have to admit the first few years are a bit of a blur to me. Although I really enjoyed it – it was too much but it all came right in the end. I'm still not the most relaxed fellow in the world and I still have a couple of tots of whisky before I go on, but not to the level I used to.

It was wonderful, after all these years of playing in the pubs, to be playing in places I never dreamed I'd ever perform in – the London Palladium, Belfast Opera House, Glasgow Concert Hall the Gaiety in Dublin – all these wonderful venues around the country, and of course, the Grand Ole Opry in Nashville.

On of my nicest memories was from the Summer Pops in Liverpool. They had a huge marquee, and I'd always had an ambition to play with an orchestra, and Ed Peak, as well as my own band conducted some of the musicians from the Liverpool Philharmonic Orchestra.

And the band sounded a bit out of tune to me and we didn't have a long time to rehearse, but come the performance it sounded fantastic – the orchestra was amazing. At the end of the night Ed Peak complimented me on my band and said how Gerry, the drummer, who was Shirley Bassey's drummer for fifteen years, kept them all together, and he was full of admiration for the keyboard player Bob Willis.

It was great, but even that night had a funny side to it. I'd hired a van from Birkenhead Van Hire and I think it had been used on a building site – it was in a sorry state. And we had these mobile homes in situ around the back of the Marquee area, and the one that I was in had previously been occupied by Tom Jones and it had all white leather furniture and a fridge and television – everything.

But at the end of the night, I'm sat on the floor of this tatty old van, surrounded by all my sound paraphernalia. So I didn't leave in quite the same luxurious surroundings as Tom Jones, but I think I had just as good a night. I certainly enjoyed the night just as much.

You often hear stories about people in this business, particularly horror stories, and I've always said that I've never met anyone that wasn't smashing. I met the wonderful Rolf Harris, and when I met him, in a passageway, after a Gerry Anderson show, he put his arms around me and said: "That was lovely that, I could have listened to that all night."

And he was lovely, singing to all the old ladies in the green room and drawing pictures for them. He was fantastic.

I met Georgie Best who was lovely. John Mill was another really nice man. Everyone I've met has been really nice, but I think it's the nature of our business that sometimes people only want to say something bad about people. I can't.

One of the highest ranking experiences I've had was the trip to Nashville. I don't know how it came about, but Granada Television made a documentary called The Road To Nashville about me, and while I was going over there I said to Mick from Ritz: "Is there any chance of me recording over there?" And he said: "Who with?"

And I said, "Jim Rooney," who did a lot of blue grass music, and funny enough he spent a lot of time in Ireland. He heard me in Galway and we had a little talk.

I told him I was a great fan and if he didn't want to do the album I would still be a fan, and he went away and the following day said, yes, he wanted to do the album. We've liked each other ever since.

He enlisted some fantastic players for the album – Gerry Douglas and Al Perkins, Don Williams' keyboard player and the fiddle player from the Nashville Blue Grass band, and Pat Mackinernie, a British drummer who plays with Nancy Griffiths. And the way it was recorded was amazing to me.

I'd first play the songs and they'd all take notes then we'd all be in different cubicles and the drummer would count them all in and it was done like that live.

And I could have just sat and listened to them playing – wonderful musicians. So we had this fantastic session and we met John Prine, who I'd been a fan of for years, and we did one of his songs. We sat on his porch till about three in the morning and sang and played and he sounded just as good on his back porch as he did on any of his albums.

We borrowed a guitar off Don Everly, and we went out to his hotel

– I think the lake is called Lake Monroe in Kentucky, and we drove up there. It's a beautiful journey where you pass things that you'd only seen on films where people were sitting on porches – and we got up to the hotel he'd arranged a big meal for us.

And then he's arranged for all these pickers to come to his back room – I think it was a dry county but he had drink in his back room – and they all played and I would have loved to stop and play, but I had to leave after dinner because I was on at the Grand Ole Opry.

On the journey back I could see signs to places that I'd heard mentioned in songs I'd sung in the Pacific Pub in Birkenhead, never dreaming I'd ever get to see them.

Doing the Opry was a great buzz – I did it three times in a week. George Hamilton introduced me. On the main night when the filming was happening, there was a circle of wood on the stage of the new Opry that was taken from the Ryman Auditorium where Patsy Cline and Jim Reeves, Elvis and everybody else had stood.

They'd planted it in the stage of the new auditorium that could hold four or five thousand people, and at the end of the night, I was one of the last on, the TV producers said I had to do it on my own because it would cost too much to film all the band.

I went on stage with my guitar and a stool in front of four thousand people, and there was a deathly silence. This could mean one of two things, but luckily I got this wonderful applause after the song, and they were fantastic to me. A couple of days later I was in Earnest Tubb's record store and the man in there asked: "Are you the English guy that's a friend of George Hamilton?" And I said yes.

He said: "Well you want to get your company into action, I could have sold a hundred of your albums in here this week, and if you multiply that by the number of places where the Opry is heard you could have had a major success on your hands!"

But it was too late – but it was a great trip.

There was a great English pub there – The Sherlock Holmes – run by an Englishman Terry and his wife Margaret. Terry had been bass player in Roy Orbison's band.

I would be in there and this big fella used to come in wearing big Hawaiian shorts, a big flowery shirt and pick up a guitar and say: "Here you are Charlie, have you heard this?" and he'd play me a song. He was the senior vice president of Sony Records.

And they had a great leaving party there for me, and this Vice President from Sony played the blues harmonica and I thought, well, you wouldn't get that in England. I found out later, when I got to know Terry and Margaret, that she'd thought I was some sort of tramp when I first walked in the pub – so much so that she'd phoned her husband who said as long as I was buying my own ale I was ok to stay.

So that was Nashville – I really wasn't looking forward to going there because I'd thought it would be all touristy and it wasn't like that at all.

There was music everywhere and the people were great and you bumped into all sorts of people, like Nancy Griffiths. She was in the bar one night with us, and some time later we saw her on our own again in a bar. She was with someone and we didn't want to disturb her – but she saw us and remembered our names and she was lovely. You can bump into anybody there. I had a lovely time there and I hope to go back. The musicians were fantastic – I was in awe of their musicianship, but they were lovely people as well and very kind to me.

Granada had lined up all sorts of gigs for me and they followed me round here, there and everywhere. Next to the English pub was a club called the Exit Inn, where I was supposed to be playing, and every time I went in the pub I could see this crowd of people waiting to get into the club, all younger people.

I thought they'd never like me and it was towards the end of the stay that I was scheduled to play there. It had a great history – all sorts of people had performed there including Barry Manilow, and lots of other great names.

And my night came, and I went backstage, and there was lots of hubbub, lots of different bands, and I was again going on alone with just a guitar. And again there was silence, but they were fantastic.

Another thing about my night at the Opry – when George Hamilton introduced me he said: "All the way from Liverpool Charlie Landsborough."

I thought if all the lads could see me now . . . and I thought I'll have to put him straight – I owed it to them. So I said: "I'm not from Liverpool, I'm from Birkenhead."

All the lads back home were delighted because we haven't got much to shout about in Birkenhead – Liverpool gets all the credit, and rightly so, so I had to say something for Birkenhead.

Even that night, a couple of Northern Irish people came to the front of the stage to say hello and I thought then how the Irish connection follows me everywhere.

It was quite like a fairy story, after all those years in the musical wilderness, when I met all these wonderful people and I started to get awards for things I wrote.

It's been a wonderful journey, and it started from a bit of desperation really when I thought my chance had gone. It's taken me across to America and I go to Australia every year, which I love.

When I first went to Australia it was coinciding with Daniel O'Donnell's tour. Daniel had been kind to me in England when he was doing his shows, bringing me on stage to introduce me to his audience, and he did the same in Australia, bringing me on stage with himself and Mary Duff.

And Australia's become one of my favourite places, I love the space, the climate, the people – I love the way there's no real class divide – I just love the place generally. I still can't speak like them though.

One nice thing I discovered is that one of my Scottish ancestors, William Landsborough, was an explorer, he went to Australia and he is recorded as being the first man to traverse Australia from the Gulf of Carpentaria to Melbourne, which is some journey, in incredible conditions. And he went off in search of Burke and Wills, who were the two explorers who went missing, and there is a Landsborough Highway, and there's a couple of town's named Landsborough.

And while I was in Brisbane I saw a Landsborough Terrace and there is a lock of William Landsborough's hair in the museum there, and there is a tree there called the Landsborough Tree where I think he had hidden provisions.

My brothers of course all sailed there, and I remember seeing a picture of Jack's Blue Funnel Line ship sailing under Sydney Harbour Bridge, and I thought that was close as I'd ever get to it.

I got there in the end, and I'm ever so thankful I did. I went to Australia, New Zealand, Tasmania – fantastic places. I was surprised, when I first went, that anybody had even heard of me, but they had. And I have great friends down there.

Music has been an incredible friend, in the places it's taken me to and the people it's introduced me to. I never dreamed it would come about and I've been lucky. I went to both America and Australia with my good Irish friend Tony Maguire, and we had a great laugh together. He looked after me well on the road. We flew economy class and we were going on board and Tony was held back.

And Thelma and I had already gone through to take our seats, and of course I was very cramped with my long legs. But Tony got an upgrade, and we had to see this scoundrel turning around smiling with his glass of vintage port.

But we had a laugh – Tony travelled in style. And I thought I was supposed to be the star!

# 19. Gentleman George

IN this great job I have now, I'm lucky to meet the people I've admired for so long.

I have been very lucky. I will never forget one occasion when the ball started rolling on a real friendship. I was playing the pubs at this time and I remember being in the house one day, mowing the lawn actually, when Thelma called out to say one of the lads was on the phone for me.

When I got to the phone he said: "Aye, Charlie, I've just been listening to the radio and George Hamilton IV was on it and he was talking about you."

Well, nobody knew me in those days and so anybody talking about me, nicely you understand, was great, but I said: "You're joking aren't you – George Hamilton – for ME?"

He said: "No, honest, he's talking about YOU.

I thought oh, he's acting the goat as we say when someone is messing around with you and winding you up. So I took no notice and went back out to mowing my lawn.

Well, the next thing the phone went again and this time Thelma comes out and she says: "Charlie, it's for you – it's George Hamilton."

Now it's Thelma so she wouldn't be having me on – would she?

I went to the phone already convinced in my head that it was somebody messing about with me again and I'm not taking too kindly to being dragged away from the relaxing task of mowing for a prank.

Anyway, this really cultured American voice says: "Hello, it's George Hamilton here."

And I said: "Oh yeah? I'm Charlie Landsborough."

But then he said something else and I thought, hold on, that's too good – nobody could put the accent on that well, that convincingly. And to my great delight it really was the lovely George Hamilton IV.

He was over in the UK doing the Billy Graham Religious Rally shows at Goodison Park – home of Everton FC – and he invited me over. I met him and it was the beginning of a long friendship and mutual respect which I value greatly.

George is an absolute gentleman, and he finished up recording a couple of my songs which was wonderful for me.

It sounds a bit of a silly story this, but when I started writing songs, George used to have his show on the telly.

George is from North Carolina, but the show came out of Canada and George sang *Canadian Pacific*, a great song. I thought even way back then George would be good to collaborate with. If I could only get one of my songs to the great man himself.

So I sat through all his programmes with a pen and paper waiting attentively for the end credits to roll to get some details where I could send a song to George Hamilton IV – but there was no address or anything like that.

I thought – that's that. It's not meant to be.

Then years later I finally met him, and he actually recorded a few of my songs. Isn't that marvellous? And he's been incredibly good to me ever since.

When nobody had ever heard of me I'd do a little gig with George somewhere, and he'd give me the most wonderful introduction, then sit at the side of the stage and listen to the whole set and come on and say even more wonderful things about me.

But that's George. He's like that with everybody – an absolute gentleman.

Another time and I was mowing the lawn again – the phone rang and this time Thelma said: "It's Ken Dodd."

This Liverpool-born funny man is a multi-talented legend in his hometown and in the UK. He is so well loved by people of all ages.

I didn't know Ken at that time – I know him now and love him to bits. He is very supportive and is always kind about me even if he does have a bit of harmless ribbing.

So this day I went on the phone and it was Kenneth Arthur Dodd – comedian, chart topping recording star and international giant.

He was talking to me about writing a song for him and he actually gave me a title to work on. The song he had in mind was called *The Might-Have Been Man* and so I wrote a song with those Ken Dodd inspired words.

He never recorded . . . the swine! I told him I'd done it and he said: "Right, I'll listen to that now."

I said: "What d'you mean?"

He said: "Sing it into the phone."

So I laid the receiver on its side and I played my guitar and sang, and he said: "That's lovely that, you know I wish I could sing like that."

He was really nice. He never did record it. But by Jove, what a day! I did get my own back in a really nice personal way when I wrote and recorded a song all about Ken Dodd and how he lights up people's lives.

I only made a few copies of a single but I did get some airplay and it was my tribute to a great man.

So as you can see, it's not been a bad life meeting my heroes and getting some really nice phone calls.

# 20. Walking on Water

I WAS with my cousin Stanley once – we were only young lads and we never had a bean – and we wanted a way of making a few bob.

So he says: "I know, the pawn shop, have you got any clothes in your house?" And I said: "Yeah, we have got stuff," (really old clothes and tatty, really antiquated, even in those days.)

"Go and get them," he said, and so we went in and got some newspaper and tied it all up, you can imagine the state of the bundle we had them in. Old Mrs Rice was passing as we had this bundle under our arm and she said: "Where are you off lads? Are you off to the pawn shop?"

Little did she know how right she was. Anyway we had to walk all the way down to town which was a few miles away, got to the pawnbrokers which was on the corner of Exmouth Street, and it was full of women with their husband's suits – I think they used to put them in on a Monday and take them back out on a Friday when they got paid or whatever.

I was standing in this line – Stanley had said: "You go in you're better at that stuff than me," and he stood by the door the coward – so I went in and waited in line with all these women and eventually I got up to the counter and this fella behind the desk said: "Yes? What is it?"

I opened this bundle, and once you got it open you'd never get it closed up again, and said: "Give us three pound for that."

"Get out," he said. "What d'you mean?" I said, and again he said: "Get out."

"Well give us thirty bob then." All these women were laughing and my face was getting redder by the minute and I quickly reduced the fee and said: "Well give us half a sheet then."

"Get out," he said. "Well can't you give us a dollar?" Still he said "Get out." And I had to bundle it all up, and the clothes were everywhere and I had to gather them up as best I could, and Stanley was laughing like hell at the door.

I went outside and I think I ditched it in an entry just around the corner. But I was so embarrassed. Stanley had a good laugh over that for ages. And we were still skint.

I thought I'd include in this chapter a couple of comical comments about my appearance. One of my favourites was when I was playing in the Isle of Man, and I came back and I looked extra Biblical at that time 'cos I had this smock-like thing on, and I think even a pair of sandals and a little bit of a tan, for once in my life.

We'd done the gig, and went back to the hotel and I got up to the bar to get a round in. As I was heading towards the bar, there was a gang of fellas there who were a bit the worse for wear, but were in a good mood, and I could see one of them saying: "Look at the state of this fella now."

So I smiled and said: "Are you alright lads, having a good time?" And he said: "Yeah, where are you from, Mate?"

Now remember this is the Isle of Man. I said: "I'm from Birkenhead near Liverpool." So he says: "Oh yeah? How did you get here? Did you walk?" And I thought this was lovely.

Another time I was in New Zealand doing a gig and this woman came up and she said, "Would you sign this for me Charlie?"

I said of course I would. And she said: "If I tell you something, you won't be offended will you?" I said: "I don't think so, love, I'm not sensitive like."

"I took a picture of you to my mother in hospital and I held it up and before I could say anything she said, 'Is that Stewart? Because he hasn't half let himself go hasn't he?'"

Which I thought was marvellous. What a put-down that was.

Another Aussie experience was when I was with an Irish mate of mine, we'd had a few drinks and we'd come out of this hotel about one in the morning or something like that – well I'd come out, he was still inside saying his goodnights to people. I was getting into a taxi outside and as I walked out of the hotel there were three Aussie drunks by the side the road. Well, two of them were deep in conversation and didn't even see me, but the third one stood there staring at me with his mouth wide open, amazed.

I smiled politely and I got in the back of the taxi, the window was down, it was a lovely hot night, and every time I turned round there was this fella with his mouth wide open staring at me.

It was getting a bit embarrassing, I'd smiled politely a couple of times and he was still there staring, and I was just waiting for my mate to come out. Eventually he stumbled forward towards the taxi and he poked his head in the window and said: "What are you doing out on a Wednesday night, I thought Sunday was your day?"

Another Biblical reference again.

I was in Cork once doing a show and a friend of a friend said, "Will you go and see a friend of ours in hospital? He's in a private ward. He'd be made up, he's a great fan."

So I said: "Yeah of course I will." I went to the hospital and I was talking to him, and one of the nurses came in and she said: "Charlie, (cos I'm world famous in Ireland) the women have spotted you, will you go and say hello to them?"

I went over to the Women's Ward and I'm walking around just passing the time of day and asking the women how they were, and wishing them well and all that sort of stuff, and I turned this corner, and this old lady had not seen me until that point.

She must have been in her eighties and her daughter, who was by her bedside, must have been in her sixties. As I turned the corner the old lady was drinking a cup of tea and she threw her tea all over the bed and threw her arms around me. And there's me getting hugged to death, and thinking how marvellous it was to be famous, and when I stepped back she said: "Who are you?" Someone said she must have thought it was the second coming. Lovely.

Well I've been all sorts over the years, because of the way I look. I've been classified as Ben Gun, Gandalf, Tiny Tim, Abraham Lincoln, and sundry Old Testament figures and everything like that.

Once when I was coming home from Australia and we were in Sydney airport, the two lads who were with me were both ahead of me in the line. And they called me over and said: "Charlie we're getting hit here for excess baggage."

I was paying for everything and it was going to cost me a few bob. I thought if they got done, I was going to get really hammered because me and my missus had really heavy cases. But when I got to the front of my line the fella never even looked at the cases – he was a young lad and he kept staring at me.

I thought well this is alright, and I never said a word about me case. And after a while he said: "Excuse me, sir, but are you the Christchurch Wizard?" Well I've been called some things in my life but I've never been called a wizard, you know. I said: "No but I'm awful glad you think I am," because my cases had just gone through and it didn't cost me a penny. Apparently the Christchurch Wizard is this character in South Island New Zealand who holds a lot of political power I think, because he sets about changing the colours of letterboxes and all sorts of things. So he'd mistaken me for him without his regalia.

My Dad could be a little bit melodramatic, and he was always down the pub with the lads because that was how it was in those days and Mam was always in the house. He'd very often come home and if he'd had a few, he'd try and sing his way out of trouble which he never did. But occasionally they'd have these arguments, and my dad could be a bit of a drama queen and he was heading towards the door and he said: "That's it. That's it. I'm going down to the dock and I'm gonna throw myself in."

Mam never said anything, but she waited until he got right near the door and she said: "Have you got your key?"

On another occasion he said: "Right. I'm gonna slit my throat now. I've had enough." And Mam said: "The razor's on the top shelf." So he never got much sympathy there, but she had good grounds I think.

It's little daft things that you remember. I remember when I was a little kid and we had the first snow fall. And you know how magical the world looks, especially when you're a kid, when the snow's falling. I made this big snowball. I was absolutely made up with it.

I carried it into the house and I put it by the coal hole, and I thought, "I'll leave that there till after."

And when I came back, and it wasn't that long after, all that was left was a pool of water on the floor. I cried cos I was only a little tiddler, you know. I cried because I thought somebody had pinched my snowball. I was stupid even in them days.

Some things about the early days weren't funny, and for anybody who lived in any sort of housing area the bane of your life were cockroaches. Now in Beaufort Road we only saw the odd one, but my sister – our Dot – got a house in Severn Street, which wasn't far from our house, but it hadn't been lived in for about six months and it had been let to go to pot.

She was married, they didn't have much and she was made up because she'd got her own house. Well this house was riddled with cockroaches, and at that particular time I was staying with her, and I was in a room with little John, my nephew.

I was going to secondary school at the time – I was about twelve or thirteen – and little John was a toddler. He was next to me in the bed and I woke up with this thing tickling my ear. I was half awake and I turned around and saw this shape on the pillow case.

And I was up like a shot because I was terrified of them. I dragged him up – he was crying – and I killed that cockroach and on the way to school after I was walking up with my little leather jerkin on and I could feel this tickling at my cuff.

I held my hand out and this thing crawled out of my sleeve, and down my hand, and I watched it crawl to the end of my fingers and drop off, and I went white 'cos I hated them – I didn't even kill it I don't think. But I got to school and the worse thing was I kept thinking all through the day if there was anything else, and how embarrassed I would be, and how would I live the shame down if anything crawled out.

Needless to say, our Dot – who was incredibly clean – was a wonderful housewife to Jim and they cleaned the house up and they disappeared. But in those early days when they had just moved in – oh it was awful.

So not a very pleasant experience.

# 21. Held to Ransom

THEN there's the story of, well, my guitar getting 'kidnapped'.

I don't think you could say stolen. I was playing in a place called the One O'Clock gun on the Ford Estate, and I'd left my stuff near the door, and when I went to leave, my guitar had disappeared.

Now I knew all the lads and they said: "Charlie no one's going to get away with that." It was a very distinctive guitar as well.

They knew no one would ever be able to bring it out, so they knew they'd get it back. And about three days later I got this call that said: "I can get the guitar back for you but it will cost you twenty five quid."

I was a bit hard up in those days but I was absolutely delighted. I think they'd just 'kidnapped' it knowing that I'd pay a few bob to get it back. They had their twenty five quid for whatever they wanted and I had my guitar back. I wasn't particularly bothered, you know.

Now I had two 4 by 12 speakers, quite long things, and one of the lads who was 'a bit the worse for wear' but a good hearted soul said: "Here I'll give you a hand with them."

Before I could say no he'd grabbed one and took it out to my old car, and he put it in the back. But he just stuck it with the soft part face down, and I had things like jacks in there and he'd put it right on top. So half of these speakers weren't working. I was in the pub this Sunday dinner with Wilf, who looked like the fellow with the turn in his eye from the silent films, you know Ben Turpin?

Lovely guy Wilf – long gone now – he was a bin man. He asked me what was wrong so I told him my speakers were on the blink.

"Can't you get them fixed?" he asked. "Well, I will when I can afford but I can't really now, Wilf," I said. "I think it'll be about a hundred pounds." He said: "I'll give you that. I've got a couple of bob saved up I'll give you that." Which I thought gave an insight into the heart of some of the people around you.

So I said: "That's fantastic Wilf, but I could never accept it. But I'll never forget it." And I didn't.

Isn't that fantastic that somebody who had next to nothing was going to give me the money just to fix my speakers? Brilliant.

Playing in the pub on a Sunday was marvellous and we always had a great house and great atmosphere, nearly all men. One of the great characters that used to come was Arthur, whose surname I never knew, a little character who we called the 'Nine stone cowboy' because he loved his country music. If I went to America I'd always bring him one of those little tie things, you know, that cowboy tie thing, or something like that back.

He came in this Sunday and the place was choc-a-bloc, but he had this little bag and in it he had a camera and a tape recorder and a piece of knotted string and a little kid's guitar, and he'd point to me and ask if he could get up and give a song, and I'd say of course.

And he'd get up and he'd always sing *I Gave My Dog To Uncle Sam* – he's the only person I'd ever heard sing it. I think it might have been an old Hank Snow song or something.

Anyway he came up to the stage and on the way gave his camera to Mickey Campbell to take a photo of him. He gave the tape recorder to someone else to tape him, and he placed the guitar, which he couldn't play, against the speakers like he was Kenny Rogers or somebody, and he stood on top of one of those soft-topped stools from the bar.

About a foot away was all the front tables full of ale and blokes and he said: "Now I am going to attempt something very difficult. I am going to spin the lariat (the bit of string) standing on one foot and sing at the same time."

And he sang *I Gave My Dog To Uncle Sam*, wobbling all over and the lads were expecting him to go over at any minute.

Occasionally he'd forget and let the string droop and then he'd remember and twiddle it a bit until he got it going again, and to cap it all, the icing on the cake was that he took his shoe off the other foot and on that foot hanging from his sock was a thread with a cardboard fish on.

What on earth that was supposed to be I don't know but there he was singing and twirling away with his leg stuck out and a cardboard fish on the end of it.

I loved that I thought it was fantastic. If the place was quiet he'd come and do a drunken dance and play the clappers and because he was such a lovable character he'd have the whole place in an uproar.

So it was great for me to see him walking in through the door because I knew he would lift the place, you know.

I played in The Schooner, as it was known in those days. The boss came and asked me would I play every Friday night? I turned up the first night with Kenny and as I'm carrying my bits in, there were about four or five fellas walking past and as one swung his arm an iron bar fell out. I thought that's a great sign isn't it?

Anyway I knew most of the lads in there and I played there for a couple of months and I think there was only one Friday that I played there that there wasn't a fight. I spent more time standing next to my gear making sure that it wasn't pinched than I did playing.

Eventually I had to say that I was sorry but as much as I liked playing I just couldn't play there. And I'm not a fighter anyway.

I went one night and all that was left of the piano was the back strut. I don't know what they'd done to the front of it but they'd ripped it to pieces. So I didn't stay there very long.

I remember someone telling me – this was after I'd left – it was a big pub with two bars and the fella who ran it, well I don't think he had any help at the time.

Somebody called from one bar, and when he went to serve them, it was all a set up – they'd be taking pictures off the wall in the other bar, and slowly but surely the place was disappearing from him before his eyes. He said a lovely line which was: "The only thing missing here is Ali Baba – I've got the forty thieves." But it was a funny place to play.

I was in a pub down in town and an old friend of mine, Charlie MacDonald, was there as well. Somebody told me a story that a few weeks before, there was a down and out boxer in the corner, and he looked dog rough, hair everywhere and unshaven, he'd been sleeping rough and drinking Meths and stuff.

Charlie spotted him and bought him a pint and called to him: "Hey Frankie come over here and get that down you. I'm going to take you home and my missus will do you something to eat."

And he took him home, and you can imagine his wife's reaction, and while his wife was cooking him something, Charlie told his son to run Frankie a bath. So Frankie got in the bath and meanwhile Charlie gave him some of his own clothes and told him that he'd get Frankie's clothes cleaned and return them to him again.

Frankie tootled off having had a good meal, and a bath, with clean clothes on and he said: "You're a saint, Charlie."

So I'm being told this story and I thought: "Well, what's that got to do with me?" But after this I had a pint with Charlie in the pub and then I offered him a lift home.

We got near his house and the road was full of cars so I stopped up the road and Charlie said: "Listen, will you come in and meet my missus, she loves you and your music."

I agreed, and we're walking down the road together and as we got up to his house and the young lad was looking out of the upstairs window, he shouted to his mother and said: "Hey Mam, me Dad's bringing another tramp home." That was me. Marvellous isn't it?

I had a succession of really old vehicles, including this old heap of an A40 van that cost next to nothing, about £40 at the time. It was hugely over-priced at that – it really was a wreck. Anyway we used to tootle around in that.

We once had this gig in Wales to go to. So we turned up in the van, and this bloke was there who had the same model of vehicle.

Now although ours was a wreck mechanically, on the outside it didn't look bad. Whereas this bloke's vehicle looked a disaster on the outside but was fine, engine-wise.

So we had a chat and we swopped keys. He knew about engines where I was definitely no mechanic. We drove back in his van.

I recall the car wings were rotting and had curled back actually like small aeroplane wings, and we came out of the Pacific pub one Sunday afternoon and Kenny's dad, a lovely little old fella, was waiting alongside the van to tell us how much he'd enjoyed the gig.

We thanked him, and got into the van. As we pulled away we realised Kenny's dad was actually running along side the van.

So I said to Kenny: "What's your dad doing? He shouldn't be running at his age!"

I wound the window down and asked him what he was doing and he said: "It's my coat – it's caught on the wing."

It really was an awful, shambolic vehicle.

The first car I got was when I was working at Robertson Thains and I bought a Beetle Volkswagon on HP (hire purchase).

Now, I'd never had a driving lesson at that time and I drove from Eastham to Liverpool in heavy Easter traffic. Quite a journey.

Thelma was in the passenger seat and a friend of mine – Vinnie Kay – was in the back. The traffic was really bad up by the Mersey Tunnel and Vinnie was terrified because I was 'kangaroo-jumping' all over the road – how I didn't get stopped I'll never know!

I don't know how I got there, but I did, and I got back, and I carried on driving from then on.

Another Beetle blunder occurred all of my own doing.

I was leaving work and this voice shouted, "Charlie!"

It was Devil Doran, the lad I'd met in the army who had joined up expecting plenty of action and ended up washing pots and pans.

So we had a chat and went for a drink on the Saturday in the pub down the road. We drank a few pints of Guinness in an hour, and I'm even more ashamed to say that I then drove home.

I drove off and I was on the motorway – there wasn't a soul about – and I tried to take this roundabout at a ridiculous speed for this little Beetle, and next thing I knew the car was on its side and I was skidding along with myself next to the road – and I remember calmly thinking: "You stupid devil."

It bumped up the kerb, some people came running over and helped me out. We got the car back on its wheels and after re-connecting the battery cables I got it going again and managed to drive home.

Thelma was not impressed, and when I told her I could have been killed, I think she nearly killed me. But the good thing – if anything good could be said of such a situation – was that the car was written off and paid for with insurance, which is just as well because I couldn't afford it.

But that Devil Doran got me into some bad trouble there.

When I think back to some of the cars I had I really do shudder, but they got me to where I wanted and needed to be.

I had a little Mini at one stage and I think even now, how did I fit everything in?

Because I had these two 4 x 12 speakers, or whatever they were, which were quite tall things – about four feet high or so, and I had my echo chamber, my guitar, my microphone stand and other bits of paraphernalia.

I used to put them all into this Mini, in addition to myself – you know it was a miracle of engineering. I should have got in the Guinness Book of records.

There was one gig I went to at the Windmill Hotel on a place called the Ford Estate, which was a smashing pub, and I remember going there on a bike. And I thought to myself, Tom Jones doesn't do this.

But it was a great atmosphere and I wouldn't have missed that for the world.

# 22. Last Orders

I REMEMBER in the pub after hours, they'd close the doors and a select few would sit there and we'd have a few more pints and I'd sing again – I just loved singing you know.

And there were about five of us, I was just singing, and the others were sat around, and one lad – Davy Hughes – said: "Look at that Charlie, even the mouse has come out to listen to you."

This little mouse had come out into the middle of the floor, and it sat with its ears up, and it never moved for what seemed like ages. It didn't just scurry off, but sat there for quite a while. And it looked lovely, I'd loved to have had a picture of it.

A funny thing in that Pacific – there was a great character called Dobby who didn't have a family, he was a friend of Cliffy Starkey and they'd always put him up.

He was always setting fire to the place and always getting thrown out. But he was good-hearted and he knighted me.

He called me Sir Charles, which was quite an honour because he only ever knighted three people in his life and they were Joe Mercer, the jockey, Frank Sinatra, and me.

I was very proud of that, and rightly so, because I remember one night Dobby was hankering after staying behind – he wanted a few extra pints. Philly Elliot, who was one of the sons of Vera, the lady who ran the pub, said: "What are you hanging round for Dobby? You're not on. Go on hop it."

And Dobby sort of shrugged and turned, and as he's walking away Philly said: "Hang on a minute, come back." Now Philly's brother Dave, who's still a good friend of mine, played the guitar.

So Philly says: "Listen Dobb, I'll let you stay behind if you knight our Davy." And Dobby just looked at him, turned around and said "Good night."

So it really was something, that knighthood that I got. And he was always defending me. There was a part of that pub called Cowards' Corner where all the old stagers stood, and Dobby would come in and say: "Oh Sir Charles is on again today."

And the others would say: "Sir Charles? Same old rubbish week in week out, we're sick of listening to him, he's hopeless." Dobby would really lose his temper you know, God bless him. They were only winding him up, going on about me all the time.

I remember coming back from a pub in Liverpool, with Dobby in the back – me and Cliffy Starkey in the front – and I was already in trouble for coming home a bit late, Thelma wouldn't have been too happy.

Dobby's got my guitar, and I'd stopped the car to let them out and he said: "Have you heard this?" And he strummed the open strings – he couldn't play a note – and he sang, "Each time I see a crowd of people . . . " and he must have gone through about fifteen songs, interspersed with this noise from the guitar.

Cliffy was making it worse by saying how marvellous it was and how he had a hidden talent. Of course this encouraged Dobby, and we must have been there for about an hour listening to him with this awful accompaniment.

The lads told me when Dobby passed away, and I went to the funeral with them.

Afterwards we all went back to the pub in Claughton village and the lads were all a bit hard up, and I had a few bob by this time because I'd had my break, you know.

I ordered a round in, and not long after I ordered another one, and this fella said: "Hey Charlie it's not your turn. You're out of order, mate." I said: "Oh. I'm sorry Joe I didn't realise."

And I turned to Cliffy and said: "You know you've got to be careful if you get a few bob, because if you don't buy anything you're a tight-fisted so and so, but if you buy too much you're a flash sod, you know. So you can't win."

Cliffy's son turned to me and said: "Charlie, you're amongst friends, be as flash as you like." I thought that was great.

But what a lovely character Dobby was. Talking of characters, I'm going back now to mention Ned Wallace, who lived next door to us.

There were so many stories about him, but I remember me and Kenny McGonagle carrying our bits and pieces in on a hot summer's Sunday afternoon and as I passed who's stood in the doorway but Ned. So I said: "Alright Ned how are you?" And he said "Oh I'm alright, but the old throat's in desperate need of some lubrication."

I said: "Oh is that right Ned?" I thought I'll let him suffer, and each time I went past he'd mentioned something else about his throat, and how dry it was. I was going to let this go on until I finally carried the last piece in, then I was going to take him in and buy him a pint, which I think I did anyway.

But Kenny came in and he was laughing and he said as he passed Ned he had given him something for his throat. He'd passed him something out of his top pocket, and when Ned looked at it – I think he'd thought it might have been a ten bob note or something – it was a Victory V lozenge.

Ned would come in to the pub regularly and Vera would sometimes let him stay in the pub overnight, but one particular morning Vera came down to find Ned absolutely blotto – he'd had a go at all the optics in the bar. So she barred him.

And on Sunday afternoons, wherever he'd been he would come

back to the Pacific, and pop his head round the door to look for me.

I was driving a gas wagon at the time and I would give him a lift home. Now on this particular day, standing right by the door was Vera. And she said to him: "You've got a nerve after what you did to me. I told you you're barred, now beat it."

Anyway, he walked around the corner to the other door, while at the same time, Vera, like it was choreographed, walked over to the same door.

And as he walked in she said "I thought I told you you're not welcome here. Beat it."

"God bless us Vera," he said, "How many ale houses do you own?" Now Thelma didn't know him like I knew him and her introduction to him came when he came over to us and I bought him a pint and gave him some ciggies.

I was giving him a lift home, and I asked him where he wanted dropping and he said: "Anywhere Charlie, you know me I can sleep anywhere, on a pavement, in a garden, it doesn't matter just somewhere up the North End."

I knew that this wouldn't be the case, he wouldn't be kipping in a garden or on the street, he'd be home as soon as I dropped him off.

So I let him out, and as I walked around the van to let him out he'd tapped Thelma, and got a few bob off her, and some ciggies.

When I got back in the van, he just lay down on the pavement, and Thelma said: "You can't leave him there." I said: "He won't be there as soon as we're gone."

I drove off home and Thelma said: "I can't sleep tonight. That poor man left there."

So I said again he wouldn't be there but I drove all the way back and when I got there, by St. James's Church, there's Ned standing in the doorway, smoking a cigarette and counting the money that we'd given him.

But you couldn't dislike him he was a cracker.

Everybody's heard the Scouse jokes about the names the Dockers gave to each other, but I thought one of the cleverest I'd heard was in the Pacific when one of the lads came in and said: "Have you seen the astronaut Charlie?"

I said: "The astronaut? Who's that?"

"Johnny Kidd."

"Why d'you call him that?" I asked.

"Because every day when work finishes he says, 'Well lads I think I'll drop in the Pacific on my way home.'" Clever isn't it?

I think it's worth recounting the little story behind my microphone stands as well.

When me and Kenny first started out, I was just playing in Ma Bush's – I think I got £1 – when Kenny came in and asked if I fancied starting a duo. So we got the old battered van, and we put the gear in and we pulled up outside The Star pub in Cleveland Street, Birkenhead.

I went in and said to the manager, "D'you mind if we practise in your bar mate?" He had all the old dockers in there and the pub was full, and he said: "Yeah alright lads."

So we went in and set up and played. It went down really well and he gave us a pound and said if we came back the next week he'd give us another pound which we thought was great.

Vera heard about us and asked would we play in her place every Thursday for a fiver.

So we thought we'd really arrived then. But in those days, I didn't have any gear at all – Kenny was the only one who had any real gear, and that wasn't much, you know.

I remember I didn't have a mic stand. For my first gig I had a chair and brush leaning against it, and taped to the top of this brush was this mic, linked to this little amp. So that was my first mic stand.

Then I got a budgie stand which I thought was great. I thought I've cracked it now, and I put a little mic on the top. And I was away.

Kenny worked down at the docks somewhere and he got a tractor wheel and cut the rim and put the mic on to that. He was a clever lad, Kenny, still is.

So I'd progressed from a broom, to a budgie stand to an upside down tractor wheel.

Then one night I was playing the Pacific and stuff was always being left there – it was a great pub for music, lots of bands played there and gear would be left around. I was setting up and I saw this new looking mic stand, and I was moving it aside thinking, "That's brand new who's left that?"

There was a card on it and it said 'To Charlie, Happy Birthday.'

And it was from friends of mine – Harry and Linda Majilton.

I've still got it to this day.

# The Stories
# Behind the Songs

STORYTELLER has been the title of one of my albums and is now
the title of this – my autobiography.

Stories are a thread in my life – from the words and music on stage
and in my songs to the background tales I use to introduce them.

I want people to know what makes me feel a certain way. A lot of
folk I know have certainly inspired my songs – or knowingly or
unknowingly they feature in them – so it's nice to mention them in
my own way.

Inspiration for my songs comes from all sorts of different places,
people and events. Sometimes I've had none at all. Sometimes I
start with an idea and halfway through come up with another that's
even better than the original. Sometimes I just do something without
thinking and surprise even myself.

I write lots and lots of stuff. Most is pretty awful, but the more
shots at the goal, the more likely you are to score. But, I never made
it as a footballer – my job is singer songwriter and I love it.

I think I've scored with the songs you will see in this
autobiographical journey through some of my material.

When I began my first attempts at songwriting I'd listen to
something I'd written and then see if I could imagine hearing it on
the radio. If it travelled. It was usually a shake of the head and back
to the drawing board. However, when I wrote *You're Still Around*
my imagination gave me a nod of approval.

Bravely, I decided I would play it in the pub at my next gig. The showcase was at the Bramley Moor pub's long bar on the famous dock road in Liverpool.

I never announced the song – fearing rejection – but when I'd finished I got a polite smattering of applause, I was delighted.

The following week as I was getting up my gear in the same tavern a little docker came up to me. He said: "Hey lad, you played a song in here last week about a ghost. It was great – would you play it for me and my missus tonight?"

He'll never know how good he made me feel, that docker.

It was the first request I'd ever had for one of my own songs and the first public response to something I'd written. I said jokingly, if he'd have been better looking I'd have kissed him. Something certainly not to be advised on the dock road in Liverpool.

Songs arrived by various methods. Some times I get a song idea when I am with friends. Take one of my favourites *What Colour Is The Wind*.

Some years back I was celebrating my birthday whilst playing a gig in Southport for an American singer-songwriter called Hugh Moffat. And during the course of the evening many of my friends arrived and brought me lovely gifts of books and CDs. Little did I realise that evening that I was to receive one of my best birthday presents ever.

You see, in the audience that night was a fine performer called Pete Naden. Pete came and sat with me and he shared a drink and it was then he told me he had heard this wonderful title for me. He said a friend of his overheard a young blind child asking her father the questions: "What Colour is the Wind?"

Pete told me that he had not managed to do anything with it so was giving it to me to see if I could. I thought then, as I do now, what a beautiful phrase. So a few nights later, I began the daunting task of composing a song worthy of that lovely title.

I was never really aware of its potential until I began to play it at gigs and get this wonderful, warm reaction. I still get it now at every show across the world.

I am forever grateful to Pete Naden and especially to this little child for the title which inspired the song that brought me the life in music I'd always dreamed of.

A few years ago my local paper focused on the song's special place in my heart and my audience's collective heart as well as its role in my life, and they asked me what colour is Birkenhead? My hometown and the place where I grew up and still live.

I said straight away: "It's gold."

Birkenhead feels like a friend which leads me on to the song *My Forever Friend*. It has its roots in my time as a primary school teacher in 'Golden' Birkenhead for 14 years. Whenever my turn for the school assembly came around I would write a little playlet around a theme and a song to accompany it. My storyline for one of these assemblies was friendship and although I'd completed the rest of the content I still didn't have a song.

Then inspiration arrived in the post, relatively speaking. My dear sister Joyce sent me a card for no particular reason – she's like that, our Joyce. Very thoughtful. You see, it wasn't even my birthday but at the bottom of the note she'd written: "To my forever friend Charlie."

I thought what a perfect title. As you can see as you get to know me better and you will in this book, you can tell how much I like and value titles – they are so important. In this case it set me going to write a song for the ultimate 'Forever Friend' – Jesus Christ.

Looking back now I can see a great little fella called Paddy Norton (he's 6ft plus now with children of his own which shows you just how long ago it was) and he sang it at the school and did it brilliantly.

I then forgot about it until years later when I was playing a country musical festival on Easter Sunday in Kessingland, Norfolk. I thought *My Forever Friend* would be appropriate and I was surprised and delighted at the response it received. I decide to keep it in my repertoire and since then it has been used at Christenings, weddings and funerals.

I also had the honour to sing it at a commemoration of the Irish Famine in a service at Tuam Cathedral, before the then Irish Taisoch and collected dignitaries from all over Ireland. This song, a simple expression of my own faith, along with *What Colour Is The Wind* was ultimately responsible for many of the good things that have happened to me. Thank you Joyce, Thank you, Lord.

I have Joyce to thank for another of my most requested songs *Love You Every Second*. That came about when Joyce bought a watch for her husband, Ken, and had this lovely phrase inscribed upon the back. What a delightful sentiment thought I and 'stole' it for my song. Clearly other people thought a lot of her idea for the watch inscription and have happily followed suit. Her idea has brought joy to a lot of loved ones and given some engravers more work – you could say 'overtime'.

Another great title is all about time too, and with someone extra special – *I Will Love You All My Life* is a ballad I can trace back to the early days of my marriage to Thelma.

I'm sure that like a lot of blokes' wives she wanted her hubby to be more of a handyman. I'm not but I do live in the same house – so I'm quite handy. To really rub it in and make matters worse for my pride she would point to my brother Jack and say: "Why can't you be more like him?"

Our Jack was much better at decorating and DIY than I ever was. I must have obviously mulled this over subconsciously a lot.

I recall driving my little Mini car to a gig in Wallasey – suddenly I sang the first line of this song, words and melody together.

Surprised at my sudden seemingly spontaneous act of creation, I realised the idea wasn't bad at all. I knew I had to remember what I'd sung – I had no tape recorder with me, so all night between songs I would turn away from the customers and sing the melody quietly to myself all the time.

When I arrived home that night I dashed to my room, and put the idea onto tape. I wrote most of the song over the next night or two but only got round to adding the chorus about 18 months later. The song, I realise, was me saying to Thelma: "Okay, I might be pretty hopeless at painting and decorating but I love you...isn't that enough?"

I believe that some songs are mulled over subconsciously and crystalise over a period of time and come out eventually.

It's a happy procedure which happened with *Last Night I Dreamed I Was In Heaven*. That took shape when I was travelling to a place called Darwen in Lancashire.

As I was driving around without thinking of anything in particular I sang the first line of this song. I quickly pulled into the car park of a Little Chef, took my guitar from the boot and on the back seat of my car I wrote down the melody line and the words I'd seemingly spontaneously sung. Prior to this I suppose I'd pondered what heaven would be like if I arrived there and someone I loved very much wasn't there.

Some folk have been a little confused by the song and ask who is the angel of the final verse. I always say, see what you think.

The life around me also inspires me and characters. Through my local church I came to know Alf Pritchard and his wife Alice – two lovely people. When Alice died, Alf was on his own and in a lot of pain due to very bad arthritis. He was a real stoic however and never complained and clung to hs home for as long as he could.

I would knock on his front door and it seemed to take an eternity for him to answer. When he did open the door and I asked how he was he would say he was fine even though I could see the pain etched in his face. When things became too difficult for him to cope with they moved him into a home - something he'd resisted for as long as he could. He wanted to stay surrounded by his memories of his life with his beloved Alice.

Not long after I was walking down his street and looked across at Alf's place. Sadly, I wondered how he would have felt if he'd been in my shoes looking at the home he'd shared so many happy years with lovely Alice. *Walking On My Memories* is me pretending I'm him. (I'm a great pretender – now there's a good title for a song.) This is my little tribute to two gentle, honest and kindly Christian souls. I think of them when I play this song and I hope it moves people the way it will always move me.

Some songs spring up out of nowhere when I am on tour away from home, such as *Look What You've Done*. I wrote that while touring Australia in 2004 and I was heading down a long highway for Melbourne – a happy memory of many happy days in beautiful Oz.

And a song called *Sentimentally Yours*, I wrote all the verses when I was travelling up the A1 between smiling for all the numerous speed cameras. The chorus I added later. Perhaps I should try the A1 again and see if the spirit moves me once more. If I take my pen for the next traffic jam on the M6 perhaps I coud write my next album.

As you can see the family is a great inspiration and one of my first musical inspirations was our Arthur.

*My Heart Would Know* is inspired by him. I used to sit enthralled when he and the lads off the ships came back for a musical session and a few drinks. He was the first in our area with a guitar and I loved listening to him sing the songs from the likes of Jimmy Rodgers and Hank Williams. Arthur was a lovely warm, kind, generous and easy-going soul and it was really sad for all of us who knew him in later life when he was diagnosed with having Alzheimer's Disease.

While it was in its early stages his wife Teresa took him to the doctors for some tests and the doc asked our Arthur if he remembered what his last job was.

Arthur looked blank and said he couldn't remember. At this the doctor thought: "Right! I'll ask another."

"Do you know what your last address was?" Arthur couldn't remember. At this the doctor said: "Don't worry you've just got a touch of er...erm....er..." and looked a bit befuddled.

Arthur looked straight at him and said, a little indignantly: "You're as bad as I am." He still had that great sense of humour I'll never forget and which I hoped rubbed off on me.

Later on, however, when it was really bad and he was in a home he couldn't remember anything – not even anyone's name. Still, when someone close to him walked in, his wife or a member of the family, his eyes would light up in recognition and a little smile would touch his face. *My Heart Would Know* has long since turned out to be a love song but it was inspired by that light in our Arthur's eyes. Something transcends ordinary memory and that thing is love.

I'll never forget our Arthur.

I am a man who likes old fashioned traditional values and I think this is a feeling that generated my song *What Happened To Love*.

This song is hankering for a return to all the old values. Sometimes nowadays it seems that those things which are most crass, crude, vulgar, loud and mean, unfairly get the most rewards. To strive for virtues seems to be considered by some as unfashionable and twee.

I think, however, that deep inside most of us is a yearning for a world where honesty, kindness, humility, faithfulness, patience and gentleness are the norm. That hunger is the thread that runs through this simple country song.

Cars have been a source of inspiration especially the ones I owned in earlier years which could only be described as 'bangers'. I seemed to be continually breaking down and forever working to repair them. I couldn't really expect anything better as none of them cost me very much. I recall one I bought for £15.

One day I was struggling with my brother-in-law Johnny to repair yet another of my old heaps. Just when it seemed it was beyond us, Johnny succeeded in doing what he'd been trying to achieve in getting the motor restarted. "Well done, mate," I said. "How do you do these things Johnny?" I asked.

He smiled and said "That's a good title for a song."

I filed the idea away in my memory and later wrote this romantic ballad called *How Do You Do These Things* which has nothing to do with cars. The great Frank Ifield rang me from London and told me that this was one of his favourite songs and that he'd had it played at his wedding. A song that came out of a very unromantic event.

Music itself has brought me some wonderful friends and some of the first people I met in the business were Foster and Allen.

Tony Allen first invited me to Ireland and we've remained the best of friends ever since. Tony is a lovely singer and had recorded a number of my songs but I have never written a song for Mick who is also a great character.

I often meet complete strangers who inspire me. *Passing Through* is about the time I was waiting at Dublin Airport for a flight back to Merseyside. I remember one particular flight landed and the passengers disembarked. Amongst the crowd passing by was an old Irish gentleman who spotted me and came over. He was very kind about my music and I thanked him and inquired if he was returning from holiday.

"No, son, he said, "I live over your side now."

"Even better," I said. "You're going home on holiday."

"Oh no," he said. "I'm going home to Limerick because my brother has just died."

I said that was a very sad reason to be going home and that he had my greatest sympathy. He smiled at me in a gentle warm way and said: "Ah son, we're all just passing through."

As he walked away I was struck by the lovely aura of kindness about him and I was left with that gentle piece of philosophy. I often wondered did he ever get to hear the song he inspired.

Talking of dear old Ireland, *Irish Waltz* was my attempt at writing an Irish song that Mick might possibly sing. In fact some 'la la' bits I thought would or could be him on his accordian. Well, he never did record it, but I liked it and went on to record it myself.

So it's still thanks to Mick for motivating me that way. The first time I ever sang it was in the front room in a friend's house – they all danced and I took that as a sign of approval. Ah, happy days.

Travelling certainly inspired me. On one drive home from Bromsgrove in the Midlands to Birkenhead I had the title *Further Down The Road* in my head. I had two songs with this title but in different ways as a musical road...the road of life or a spiritual road or maybe they are all intertwined...like a lot of my songs, dear reader – you decide.

Music is very much a two-way affair and without the audience the experience simply wouldn't be complete.

# An Audience with ...
# Charlie Landsborough

---

CHARLIE is always a joy to interview as those who meet him from press and broadcasting media can confirm.

He is often asked questions right across the board. Now, for the first time, he sits down with a pint of Guinness and answers some of the most asked posers about his life and personal tastes. This is the low-down on Landsborough.


Charlie, you have covered many Beatle songs and medleys on your albums and tours. Why are they so special and do you have any favourite songs that remain with you?

I am a huge Beatles fan and consider them to be the best band ever.

The creative output of John, Paul, George and Ringo is second to none. It's difficult to pick a favourite song, there are so many: *Across the Universe*, *Come Together*, *Lady Madonna*, *In My Life*, *Strawberry Fields (Forever)* – I am afraid it is a case of etc etc etc.


Who is your all time favourite singer male and female?

This is so difficult to pick one of each, but if pushed here's a few of my favourites. Ladies first – Jennifer Warnes, Dolly Parton, Jo Stafford, Eva Cassidy, and Kate Wolf. For the men it would be Elvis, John Prine, Jim Reeves, Bing Crosby, David Gates, Bob Dylan and Michael Buble.

You relax by watching telly: what is your all time favourite TV programme?

It is the British sitcom Ever Decreasing Circles, which ran from 1984 to 1989 and starred the very versatile Richard Briers and Penelope Wilton. Richard Briers played Martin who liked to be in control of everything but it seldom turned out that way in the end.

Do you have any favourite films that you always go back to?

Captains Courageous, a seafaring film starring Spencer Tracey, and the classic feel-good film It's A Wonderful Life starring James Stewart.

You are a well-read man. What is your favourite novel or biography or good old fashioned read?

John Steinbeck's Short Stories.

In the course of your travels you met a lot of people who gave you advice. What would you say is the best piece of wisdom shared that you have been given? Do you stick to it?

My advice is 'Be Yourself!' And do I adhere to it...? Yes, eventually.

Do you have a Charlie Landsborough motto in life?

The family motto is 'Fear God & Fight' from my Scottish ancestry, which is rather comical for a pacifist like me – I'd probably drop the last two words.

You tour a lot so are you into this new fangled world of mobiles, emails, Twitters and ipods?

No, not at all!

You work hard – so where would you go for a holiday?

Australia – Scotland or Ireland with sunshine.

Now this is a tough one , What is the best concert you have been to apart from your own?
Ry Cooder at the Apollo in Manchester. Marvellous.

Are you superstitious?
Not anymore although at one time I always liked to have something red about my person.

Are you a fan of Christmas and all it entails?
Yes and No. Yes because I love my Saviour and also the family aspects of Christmas. No because I dislike the hype and falseness of much that transpires at that time.

What is your biggest regret?
That I've made so many mistakes, that I was not kinder to my dad and also that I didn't turn up for a gig, when the band I was in were sharing the stage with The Silver Beatles.

What ambitions do you still have?
To write a song with the timeless quality of say *Stardust* or *Beautiful Dreamer* and to sing a duet with Dolly Parton or Willie Nelson.

How important are your fans to you?
Incredibly important – I owe them everything and many of them are now great friends.

What role do your management team, band and fan club have in your success?
You never achieve anything alone and I have a wonderful team of people around me who help make what I do such a pleasure. Ken Davies my manager has been a huge influence, my sister Joyce works so tirelessly, my band Tony & Pete Ariss, Pete Brazil, Gerry

Freeman, Jason Forrester, Karl Benson, who bring my songs to life.

Pete Ware who has been the creative producer on most of my recordings, Nikki and Bob Benson & family who do a fantastic job with our fan club and not forgetting our sound & lighting crew from AdLib who are not only great at their work, but also a delight to be around. Mustn't forget John Smith who oils the wheels of our travels with laughter and our Jamie and Pete the Hat for their priceless contributions.

When you finally get to meet Jesus (we all hope it's a long, long way off) you are allowed one question – what would it be?
Are my family and friends here?

Have you ever seen a ghost?
No, but I've looked like one on occasions.

What do you think of reviews of your shows? Do you read them, take notice or ignore them?
Because I'm not the most confident of people, it's always good to read a positive review – everyone needs a pat on the back sometime. Someone once called me a singing tree which only made me smile. If that's as negative as it gets I don't mind.

What famous person has most impressed you?
George Hamilton IV. He is gracious, selfless, humble, generous, kind and a great servant of the Good Lord.

What are your strengths and your weaknesses?
My strengths, I suppose, are my faith, my ability to laugh at myself, and honesty and hopefully humility. I have much to be humble about. My weaknesses are indecisiveness, a desire to please everyone, occasional self-righteousness and self doubt.

What do you miss most when touring?
My grandchildren, my own bed and my home town.

You love to tell a good tale and listen to them – the art of a true
Storyteller. So when did you last cry laughing?
Last night, recounting a story of a POW who desperately wanted to
learn French and had no language to trade with. He told a fellow
POW who was desperate to learn Chinese that he would teach him
in exchange for French lessons.

Although he knew no Chinese he made up a language of his own
and proceeded to teach his friend this gobbledygook.

The trouble was his friend was brilliant and rapidly assimilated
all he was taught. In the end the poor chap teaching him was having
to stay up all night inventing more rubbish and also having to learn
it himself. He dreaded meeting his 'Chinese' student as he'd be in
the washroom and hear Ah Choi Ping Soo and have to remember
what it meant and also to respond appropriately. He had not time to
learn any of the French the other man was teaching him.

In the end the stress began to tell and he had to tell his student the
awful truth. The man upon hearing that he'd spent weeks learning
absolute gibberish was enraged and chased him round the camp
threatening to kill him!

Do you believe that we make our own luck?
Yes, as Gary Player the golfer once said: "The more I practice the
luckier I get."

If your house was burning down (God forbid) what of the following
would you save (apart from Thelma). OK Charlie?

Photograph
Picture of me with my mum and me with Thelma as a girl.

Something from the house gold disc/souvenir
A painting of my mum and dad our Doreen had done for me in the US.

One of your own records
*What Colour Is The Wind* as that's what started it all.

Religious
My bible

Musical instrument
My old Martin guitar

Piece of clothing
My linen suit tailored by my dear friend Attilio Marchini and his wife Pam.

Is there anything you want to get off your chest?
Yes my seven hairs, they're neither one thing or the other and they're turning grey. On a serious note the PC (Politically Correct) brigade drive me mad. And I hate people who are cruel to animals.

What is your ideal night out?
My ideal night would be to hire a hotel and gather all my family and friends and all the many wonderful characters I know from all parts of my journeys and see the interaction, hear the music and laughter and bask in the warmth of it all. On a realistic level it would simply be a night in a local pub reminiscing and laughing with old friends.

What do you think of talent shows?
Not a lot.

What was the best compliment you have had, either spontaneous or by a fan?

The old lady in Strabane who said: "You don't listen to you with your ears son, you listen with your heart."

You are a proud supporter of Liverpool Football Club – what is your favourite memory of The Reds?

Liverpool coming from behind to beat Milan in the European Cup.

Have you ever met someone you deemed a 'living saint?'

I met a beautiful older nun in Ennis in Ireland who had this wonderful radiance and aura of goodness and serenity. She was truly beautiful in a spiritual sense – you could almost touch the purity in her.

You are often mobbed when you come off stage for autographs, can you remember the first one you signed?

Yes, I was in Germany and felt a little embarrassed and thought that perhaps the person was taking the mickey as I wasn't famous. They weren't – which was lovely.

You are very, very proud of your roots. How would you describe the place you came from?

Like an old friend, a little unkempt and eccentric, but whom you love for his warmth, lack of pretension, humour and generosity – despite all his other failings.

What is your biggest phobia?

Heights and dying . . . in reverse order.

If you had to say one thing about your career what would be the highlight?

Topping the Irish Charts in 1995!

If they made a film about your life who would play you?
**Ricky Tomlinson or Billy Connolly.**

What character in literature can you most relate to?
**Don Quixote.**

There is a lovely upbeat and celebratory song called *Blessed* by Joan Armatrading. Do you think you have been blessed?
**Yes, God has blessed my life with the gift of music, and wonderful family, great friends and the promise of eternal life through his Son Jesus Christ.**

You are given one 50p to play only one song on a jukebox containing every song in the world – what would it be?
*Hurt* **by Johnny Cash.**

If you had not made it big what do you think you would be doing now?
**Complaining! No, seriously, I'd still be writing and playing in some capacity.**

You have won plenty of musical awards. Do any in particular stand out in your memory?
**I love them all – they are special recognitions that people care about what you do. One of my favourites was a unique honour from the undisputed King of Comedy – Ken Dodd.**

**I am in a rare breed of recipients of a much sought after Golden Clap Award. On the certificate signed by the great man himself it was presented to me in Liverpool at one of Ken's exclusive Good Turn Society Lunches.**

**The citation reads: "To Charlie Landsborough for being a 'Bacon' in the entertainment world." I told him that I thought it was a**

mistake and should have said: "Beacon", He patted me on the head and said in that wonderful voice: "I'll be the judge of that, Son."

So not that many people have it in writing like me. I have the clap it's official – it's framed at home and is quite a conversation starter.

Another prize was equally memorable but for a different reason. I recall being well chuffed at getting my first music award and deciding to go along to pick up my prize in person. It was very early in my career. So I went along and did a short set in this little club in Liverpool. After the showcase, my Thelma went to the Ladies Room and in there this woman she'd never met said: "Isn't he bleedin' dreary?"

You come across as a very modest type of guy. How come fame and all that goes with it hasn't affected you?

Well, I live in a better house than I ever dreamed I would own, I'm now able to look after my family better and I travel much more than I ever did, but I still live in the same area and still have all my old friends and still go to the same old places so some things haven't changed at all - thank goodness. My family keep my big feet firmly on the ground. One thing that has changed dramatically is the type of venue I now play and the great support I have. There's no more carrying my own gear in and out of pubs.

What are the things you love about life?

The simple things – tea, bacon and eggs. Characters and eccentrics, humour, pubs, laughter. Animals and my grandchildren.

Accents such as my native Scouse. The Geordie and the Scottish especially. I love honesty and humility in equal measure. Musical instruments, clocks, art craftsmanship, photography, beer and whisky. Twilight, oh yes. My family and my study at home. I love the sound of water – the sound of water running – rivers, lakes, canals, always gets to me. Oh and my forever friends.

And finally, there are some wonderful stories in this book,
but what has been the most bizarre? Give us one for the road ...
Whilst in the Army in Celle and out for a night on the town with the
lads we would often finish up in "Der Teufel" (The Devil) strip club,
simply because it was the only place you could get a late night drink
– honest!

One night a group of partially dressed dancers were doing the
introductory entertainment before the strippers came on. One of
these dancers kept dancing toward me and fixing her gaze on me.

The lads said "You jammy devil Scouse, she really fancies you."
I never made a move but I remembered and the following week I
visited "Der Teufel" on my own and a bit earlier.

As I entered at the door, there to greet me was the dancer in
question. I asked if she would care to join me for a drink to which
she agreed. After a couple of drinks she said: "I'm not what you
think I am you know." I thought she meant that because she was a
dancer, that she was not of easy virtue.

I said: "I think you're jumping to conclusions – as far as I'm
concerned you're just a lovely young woman and that's good enough
for me!"

She replied: "Well I'm not." I was a bit bemused but replied:
"Well, okay then, if you want flattery you're a lovely young girl."

She replied: "I'm not."

I said jokingly: "Well you're the strangest looking man I've ever
met." Imagine the shock when the response came: "Well I am!"

I finished my drink and left. I'd never met a man before that
looked completely like a woman – he certainly fooled me and the
rest of the lads.

When I got back to camp and told them they fell about laughing.
I wasn't amused!

# Forever Friends
## Stories About the Storyteller

---

The Wizard of Oz
By Roger Lyon
BBC broadcaster

WHEN I was living in Australia in the mid 1990s I worked at a radio station in Newcastle NSW called 2NUR.

They had picked up on *What Colour is The Wind* and had started playing tracks from Charlie's album to great response from their listeners. I returned to Liverpool and BBC Radio Merseyside in 1997 and shortly afterwards met and interviewed Charlie for the first time. I told him about his popularity in Australia and I distinctly remember telling him that he should try and arrange a tour Down Under. He seemed a little unsure, but I had no doubts that he would be very successful there.

Sure enough, several tours later, a Charlie Landsborough ticket is hot property in Oz, and not only that, but I know that Charlie has also fallen in love with the country. On a personal note, my stepfather John, had always been an avowed Johnny Cash fan – until he heard and fell in love with Charlie's music. From that day he was a convert. Although a Liverpudlian, he had emigrated to Australia in 1982. In 2004, on what was to be John's last trip back home, I arranged for him to come in and sit in with me on my Late Show on a night when Charlie was to be my special guest.

You would have thought that he had won the Lottery.

Charlie was a true gentleman and was very happy to answer John's questions and treated him like an old friend.

When Charlie started touring Australia, one of the regular dates on his itinerary was at a club in Hexham, just outside Newcastle and as I was holidaying there at the time, I bought tickets and arranged for John to meet Charlie backstage before the show.

At the time John had been diagnosed with a form of Leukaemia and was having treatment. When he met Charlie in the dressing room, and shared a tot of the 'hard stuff' with him, it was as if all his cares and worries had been lifted from his shoulders.

Charlie was truly kind and caring and I know that when we left to watch the show, John's impression of Charlie had gone even higher than it had previously been.

Sadly John passed away in August 2005 and at his funeral, Charlie's *My Forever Friend* was played. Every time I have seen Charlie since then, he always recalls his meetings with John and is never without a kind word. Aside from being a very talented singer and songwriter, Charlie is a genuinely nice man. There is no side to him and what you see is what you get.


The Birkenhead Cowboy
By Billy Butler
Former Cavern DJ, Television and Radio Star

SUCCESS hasn't changed Charlie – neither has Jack Daniels.

From the Pacific pub to the Palladium Theatre he's stayed the same guy – warm emotional and real. I'm proud to have played his stuff for years – even the ones he hoped I didn't have. I gave him his first Empire Theatre booking , but forgot to tell him – thank god he heard it on the radio.

Success deprived us of a great Buffalo Bill tribute act.

Prize Asset
By Maureen Walsh
BBC Radio Merseyside

CHARLIE Landsborough gives those of us who cannot put our feelings into words, songs that convey messages for all our listeners.

His heart and soul are laid bare in his performances.

He projects so much love and affection. Is it any wonder audiences respond to him as they do? Hearing Charlie on BBC Radio Merseyside has created many fans which reflects in my escalating postbag when giving away a Charlie Prize.

Shake Those Pots and Pans
By Bernie Green
Friend

SOME time in the 60s the band I was in decided to become a five piece. Frank Wan, our steel player introduced Charlie.

We all agreed he was right for us. He suited our sense of humour, could sing and harmonise well. We would practice in Eddie Clayton's house. At break time we would retire to the kitchen where Eddie's wife Joan would fix us a cuppa of tea.

Charlie always stayed in the living room singing – unbeknown to Charlie we would be listening to him, and he would sing several songs (to his unseen) audience before we would resume practice.

Still unknown to Charlie this became a regular occurrence. He was as easy to listen to in Eddy's kitchen as he is in the Philharmonic Hall. I'm still listening to Charlie.

## Mystical and Magic
By Paddy Weir
Friend

I FIRST met Charlie in 1964 when we were pals in the army.

Roll over Beethoven and the first lines of the Isle of Innistree were my best memories of Charlie singing.

From the night he sang *What Colour Is The Wind* on the Gerry Anderson Show, and every appearance here in Belfast, he always takes time no matter how busy to meet and chat with me.

His voice is mystical and magical – every song he writes has a great meaning.

## He Shines Like a Beacon
By Richard Spendlove, MBE
BBC Producer & Presenter, (South East of England)

I'VE known 'Charles Alexander Landsborough' as I always call him, for many years, and, as time has passed, it has been my privilege to watch him grow to incredible and wholly deserved stardom.

In an industry which is most definitely not noted for compassion and sincerity, Charlie shines like a beacon, both in his music and in his persona, before almost anyone else I have ever met or worked with.

Much of this almost certainly has to do with his deep-rooted Christian beliefs, which, again – generally – nowadays are so often conspicuous by their absence.

He is most justifiably adored by hundreds of thousands of fans worldwide, and – quite simply – doesn't have an equal.

On a String and a Prayer
By Billy Maher
BBC Radio Merseyside

CHARLIE has a god given talent for writing and singing songs but I've always thought his greatest gift was his sincerity.

He means what he says and we all know it, he's been a regular on my programmes over the many years. I remember with pride the day he sang from a crumpled piece of paper that newly written song *What Colour Is The Wind*, and the occasion that I opened a few of his hometown concerts with my banjo. One of my listeners tells the story of how she woke after a big operation and the first person she saw was Charlie who just happened to be visiting the local hospital.

She thought she was in heaven. There's not many of us who could be mistaken for God is there?

A Capital Guy
By Lew Baxter
Author and International Newspaper Journalist

TO hear the name Charlie Landsborough, then see this smiling face, flowing silver locks, and you can think of only one thing – warmth.

Charlie Landsborough is a versatile musician who is at home in the best musical cities: Nashville, Sydney, Dublin, Belfast, Glasgow, Cardiff and his beloved Liverpool – and the show would be the same but different. He is the best sit-down musician in the business.

A storyteller indeed who makes you feel part of the evening.

This is one of the world's greatest intimate performers and in all my years of writing about music the name Charlie Landsborough is synonymous with courtesy, laughter, poignancy and above all else great musicianship. He's a real bonnie Prince that Charlie.

## A Match Made In Heaven
### By John and Hazel
### Fans and Friends

WE have watched and listened to Charlie in pubs particularly with the great Kenny McGunigall during the early seventies.

Now he is famous we catch him at least twice a year on his tours.

From his days at the Pacific there was a lovely couple who got a little drunk throughout the day, always requesting *How Great Thou Art* on Sundays, but sadly would fall asleep for the duration of every Charlie ballad, only to be dragged into reality by the rapturous applause of the pub audience – only to fall into a deep sleep again when he sang his next song.

Whilst playing in the Windmill one Sunday he seemed, or was, ignored by a family reunion gathering, and in desperation we suggested he sing *God Save The Queen*. His faithful half-dozen loyal followers immediately stood up for the duration, sadly nobody else took a blind bit of notice.

Our memories will follow us to the next world, especially the Pacific Pub regulars, Cliff Starkey's sleight of hand, Johnny Rainer's comedy dancing and harmonies, the Landsborough percussion section, Fred on spoons, Ray on 'hand clap' and so many more too numerous to mention. Our greatest personal achievement was to be on Vera's 'stop back list' every Sunday, which played havoc with Monday's work schedules.

Alas, fame stole our salvation from under our noses. Have we any regrets? Not one. Finally back in 1996 we went to see Charlie perform at the Gaiety Theatre in Dublin along with his lovely sisters-in-laws and a host of friends. We sat in the middle of the circle surrounded by lovely Irish people – every single one of them sang with Charlie on each of his own songs. Some cried when he drifted into *Fireside Dreams* – we sat there speechless.

As a last word, many of you have heard Charlie mention 'Car Park Alf' well we have met him. And we met through Charlie's Music.

Hazel was actually sitting on my stool one busy Sunday, but I forgave her. Our friendship blossomed to marriage in 1998.

## Heart and Soul
By Seamus and Christina Kelly
Fans and Friends

A FEW years ago, in my home town of Moate, County Westmeath, I discovered the very talented Charlie Landsborough.

After a day boating on the Lordly River Shannon my wife Christina and I were strolling down Main Street when this tall bearded man resembling our saviour Jesus Christ passed by and then entered the bar famously known as The Elbow.

I remarked to Christina: "I'm glad I'm not going there."

But how wrong can a person be. Out of curiosity I along with Christina, went back to The Elbow and I'm sure glad we did, because seated in the corner of that small Irish bar surrounded by accordians, banjos and a bottle top rhythm section was the Christ-like figure weaving his magic in front of an enthralled collection of music lovers.

Not since I heard my lifetime hero Bing Crosby in youthful days was I so impressed. A genuine talent performed songs from the heart and soul effortlessly, and I like the others was becoming a faithful follower – which I still am. I made an arrangement to meet the one I call The Great Man. Charlie proved a revelation telling me all about his early family life days, love of music and his Christian beliefs. I learned a lot about humility that day, and I'll cherish evermore the memory of a couple of hours that passed all too quickly in the company of one I can truly call a real human being.

Roaring With Laughter – Weeping Buckets
By Sue Smith
Fellow Student Teacher

I FIRST met Charlie when we went to teacher training college in 1976. We were in the music department together and everyone including the lecturers appreciated just how talented this man was. He just happened to mention that he played in the pubs at weekends so my friend and I went to see him at the Talbot in Oxton.

Charlie played anything and everything brilliantly, from Bob Dylan to George Formby. My family and I became instant fans.

He could also charm the birds from the trees. Coming in very late to college one Monday morning looking the worse for wear, he said he'd been out all night looking for his dog. I don't think he even had a dog at the time but he got away with it.

After leaving college we ended up teaching at the same school for many years. In the early days we'd have some cracking arguments in the staff room, usually about religion or politics.

Charlie also used to regale us with hair-raising stories from his army days and his experiences playing around the pubs and clubs.

If he hadn't have been a musician he could have been a comedian although the people who attend his concerts already know he is.

He is also a wonderful artist. Charlie could sell the doodles he used to make during the weekly staff meetings and everyone's name had an anagram. I've yet to find out what mine was.

When his career in Ireland was taking off, Charlie had gone over there for New Year. First day back at school in January – no Charlie! Everyone is wondering where he is – eventually a phone call … the sea's too rough and the ferry can't sail.

It was probably the finest Christmas weather we've ever had and the sea was like a millpond, but again the Landsborough magic worked its charm. This was only one of the many weird and wonderful excuses he'd come up with when he didn't show up for school. They were never really lies, just bending the truth a little. I don't think the headmaster knew what to do with him.

Being a primary school we all had to take turns doing class assemblies. Charlie's were always eagerly anticipated because we knew we'd be roaring with laughter one minute and weeping buckets the next. Some of his finest songs were written for those assemblies.

When he finally became successful enough to leave teaching all together, he was missed enormously by everyone.

Whenever I meet any of the children, many of whom are parents themselves now, they always ask, about Mr Landsborough and talk about how brilliant it was being in his class.

If only all teachers had that effect on kids. What a joy to see Charlie's fabulous and well deserved success.

Along life's journey there are very few people we meet who make a positive and lasting impression on us. I'm glad to say that Charlie, musician, poet, comedian and general 'Nutter' is one of these people and I feel privileged to call him a friend.


Melancholy Maestro
By Pete Price
Comedian and Broadcaster

I FIRST heard Charlie sing at the funeral of Liverpool actress Gladys Ambrose.

I didn't know what to expect. Then I heard this lovely voice echo throughout the church. It hit me – the genuine melancholy in that voice. It remains one of the most significant musical moments in my life. I always feel better after meeting Charlie. I just wish I had his faith. It is an honour to even be mentioned in this wonderful autobiography of a man I truly admire and respect.

Bear Necessities
By Jimmy McGovern
BAFTA Award-winning Scriptwriter

I FIRST met Charlie in January 1976 when the two of us began teacher-training at the Ethel Wormald College.

We hit it off immediately. We were both skint and we had families to bring up and we were deadly serious about becoming teachers but that didn't stop us having a laugh. It was impossible NOT to have a laugh because Charlie was – is – one of the world's funniest men.

I remember him telling the polar bear joke – a young polar bear going round to all his family and asking them to reassure him that he really is a polar bear and not a grizzly or a koala or whatnot.

The little polar bear eventually gets to his granddad who asks him why he is seeking all this reassurance and the little polar bear goes, "I'm bloody freezing."

Well, Charlie told that joke to perfection. I'd watch him telling it to others. I'd watch him nearing the punchline and pulling this sad baby-polar-bear-face (I kid you not: he could make himself look like a baby polar bear) and then he'd hit the punchline and whomever he was telling it to would go into hysterics – real hysterics. A wonderful, natural comic.

Charlie (a committed Christian) started off doing RE at the Ethel Wormald but soon changed to Music, telling me that he was "a bit of a singer."

I told him I was a bit of a writer and I showed him something I'd written. He was so kind about it, so encouraging. He's probably forgotten it now but I never shall. Charlie turned out to be something more than "a bit of a singer." He turned out to be a huge, stonking success. So well done, Charlie, you warm, humble, compassionate, funny man. Well done, mate.

# Encore: The Outro

WELL, that's my story. But dear reader it's not over yet – oh no!

I've smiled and sighed inwardly as I've recounted all the many nuances of my generally happy life. I'll be forever thankful for all the wonderful people, family and friends, who helped shape what's happened to me.

People need to be inspired by their dreams and I believe that if you want something bad enough you can achieve it.

Trust in your dream and trust in the Almighty – I did.

I hope I am someone that people from all walks of life can look at and listen to and say: "If Charlie can do it after so many ups and downs then I have hope too."

I thank my Lord and Saviour Jesus Christ who's blessed me in so many ways, and who has, during the course of my life, wrought so many changes in me.

I know he's got a bit of a job on his hands, as he continues to mould me in his will.

I hope you enjoyed the journey almost as much as I have.

And I thank you for coming along.

God bless you . . . but remember, the ride's far from over . . .

*Charlie*

# Thank You
## *From The Bottom Of My Heart*

I WISH to thank the following people for their contribution to my success, for being an inspiration, for colouring my life, or simply for being my friend.

John and Carol Wyburn, Ray and Sue Waller, Malcolm and Rita Clitheroe, Paul and Barbara Brassey, Terry and Mary Lennon, Sue Smith, Johnny Rayner, Terry Connell, Gillian and David Prescott, Graham Barnes, Vera Elliott, Pat and Eilish Claffey, Tony Allen, Mary O'Sullivan, Mike Perry, Neil Coppendale, Tony Maguire, Paddy Nolan, Terry Bradford and Susie Arvesson, Maureen Allen, Liam Kennedy, Gerry Freeman, Pete Ariss, Tony Ariss, Pete Brazil, Jason Forrester, Bob Willis, Andy James, Gary Cotton, Frank Hambelton, Ian Robertson, Kenny Cumming, Gerry and Pauline Marsden, Ricky and Rita Tomlinson, Jimmy and Eileen McGovern, Ken Dodd, George Hamilton IV, Jim Rooney, John and Sheila Smyth, Pete Arthur, Car Park Alf and Margaret, Heather, Steve, Debbie and Richard, Mark Robinson, Attilio and Pam Marchini, Brian Hart, Brian Mongey, Jeff Ryan, Daniel O'Donnell, Rita and Ray Foster, Sadie and Susanne Raeside, Mary and Heather Coulson, Alf and Beryl White, ad lib, Phil McDonough, Trionagh Moore, Adam Maples, Terry Gordon, Pete Figures, Rod Coe, Mike Kerin, Jeff Mercer, Arthur Laing, Evelyn

Clements, Ann Clerkin, Ray Clerkin, May Clerkin, Pete and Tara Ware, Pastor Paul Epton, Charlotte, Ian, Jean, Andrew, Jackie and Alan, Bob and Beth Dick, Paddy McIntyre, Pat McDonnell, Ralph Norton, Harry and Linda Majilton, Liz and Michael Norberg, Shaun and Jane Michael, Eileen and the Class Girls, John and Hazel Bailey, Tea Bag June and her Gang, Bernie Green, Terry Wood, Meg and Brian Nicholson, Sharon Herbison, Joan Gartland, Frank Ifield, Ginger McCain, Dave Rowland, Mary of Downton, Geoff Denton, Paddy and Eileen Wear, Joe Betts, Sean Coyle, Jim Donaldson, Richard Spendlove, Highfield Primary, Logans Primary and, of course, my family and Thelma's family.

And there's more . . . Special thanks to my manager and mentor Ken Davies, my sister Joyce for all she does, to Nikki and Bob Benson and family for all their wonderful work with the fan club, David Smith for all his support and friendship, to my friend Mick Clerkin who played such a huge part in my success, to Thelma for staying by me through it all, for Cathy and Geraldine Roberts for backroom support. And last – but not least – to my good friend Peter Grant, who has worked so hard to gather all my verbal meanderings into one cohesive and meaningful whole ... much credit to you my friend.

I have enjoyed the support and subsequent friendship of many of those who work in the media – presenters and journalists in television, radio and print. Mick Clerkin and David Smith and all the staff at Rossette Records, Ray Levy ( ex Telstar). Gerry Anderson and Pat Kenny for lighting the initial flame. Grace and Lloyd Lakin; Robert Margaret and Marion, Linda and Stefan, Luke Bowers and Kenny McGunighall. Hugo Duncan, Ian Walker, all the theatre managers.

A thank you to the following radio presenters: Alan Watkiss and Bob Preedy, Alex Hall, Rob Underwood, Anna Bartlett and Francis Finn, Bill Rennells, Bob Brolly, Mick Ord, Billy Butler, Billy Maher, Roger Lyon, Maureen Walsh, Norman Thomas and Monty Lister, Brian Mann and Steph Lambert, David Bradley, David Spencer, David White, Duncan Warren and Emma Lloyd, Dianne Oxberry, Corrine Hill, Lawrence Mann, Ed Douglas, Mike Powell, Pauline Cox, Steve Cherelle and Eric Hall, Franca Martella and Irene Seggar, Frank Wappat, Kathy Seker and Michael Poulter and Sam Harris, Geoff Barker and Sandy Martin, Gerry Byrne and Ian Pearce, Helen West and Henry Beer, Henry Wymms, James Bursey, Jonathan Witchal and Steve McCormick, Joe Fish and Ted Robbins, John Hellings, Keith Skues, Kriss Carpenter and Marie Critchton, Mark Seaman, Richard Spendlove, Sally Meeson, Richard Cartridge, Paul Braithwaite, Matthew Davies, Roy Waller and Wally Webb, Trevor Fry, Veronica Capaldi, Shane O' Connor, Andrew Smith and Lynn Walli-Eade, Krissi Carpenter, and Mark Seaman, Liz Neeson, Maggie Macnaughton, Moira Miller, Paul Bedford, Sandy Watt, Stephen Romaine, Stuart Cameron, Stuart Fenwick, Tom Clarke-Hill and Bill Black, Tom Ferrie, Tommy Truesdale, Dave Walker, David Allan, Dean Wilding, Dick Barrie, Evelyn Queen, Helen Macpherson, John Irons, John Matthews, Karin Ingram, Ken McCleod, Pete Price, Ray Grundy, John Hannam, Phil Roberts.

And to all absent friends. I will be forever grateful to them all, and those I am yet to meet, for helping me achieve my dream.

# A Message from
# the Fan Club

BOB and I have had the privilege of running Charlie's fan club for a couple of years now, and during that time we have spoken to many people who think the world of Charlie.

It's true to say that he is a true gentleman and he's also a very humble and down-to-earth person who has never let his fame change him.

We know that is why he is so loved by all who meet him.

But, for Bob and I, Charlie is a special friend and a person who we are very proud to be associated with.

Charlie, you probably don't realise this – but everyone who knows you, speaks so highly of you, not only musically, but also of your warmth and kindness and the fact that you never fail to deliver a comforting word or two to someone in need.

People never forget that, and to be honest if I had a penny for everyone who said that to us we'd be extremely wealthy! You're not just 'International Singer/Songwriter' Charlie Landsborough, you are Charlie Landsborough 'Friend'.

Thank you for your friendship and the wonderful gift of music that you share with each and every one of us.

God Bless you Charlie. You're MARVELLOUS.

Love 'n' hugs,
Nikki and Bob

## The Charlie Landsborough Fan Club

Anyone, UK and overseas, who requires any information
about Charlie's official fan club, can contact Bob or Nikki on
01270 560226
or email ziwpip2@talktalk.net
or write to: Fan Club H/Q, 41 Jesmond Crescent,
Crewe, Cheshire, CW2 7NJ

Alternatively an application form can be downloaded
and printed off at Charlie's website at
**www.charlielandsborough.com**

Upon joining the fan club, new members will receive a
special welcome pack which includes a membership badge
with a unique membership number, a calendar, key ring, fridge
magnet, several of the official fan club button badges, stickers, a
biography and info sheets including a merchandise list.
After this each member receives a quarterly newsletter.

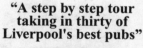

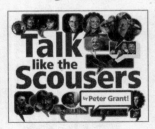

Music runs in the family as Jamie sings
and Charlie strums along

Back to school: Marvellous! In the spring of 1995 after I'd left teaching and got my big break

Mine host: Me and Vera Elliot, boss of the Pacific Pub

The craic: Tony Allen, Thelma, me and Sean Shannon in West Meath, to be sure

Prine time: The one and only John Prine, Thelma and me

Pride and joy: The legendary Charlie Pride and another Charlie

Irish superstars Daniel O'Donnell, Mary Duff and Dominic Kirwan join me at Frinton Free Church in December 1999

From the River Mersey to the Canadian Pacific: Me and 'gentleman' George Hamilton IV

Old friends: The legendary Foster and Allen

Tee for two: A round of crazy
golf with Ricky Tomlinson

Above right: He's always on the
minds of music fans – honoured
to be with Willie Nelson
Right: With Ken Dodd

FASHION'S GREAT COATS | TIM ROTH — HOLLYWOOD'S MAVERICK TALKS

RTÉ GUIDE

IRELAND'S LARGEST-SELLING MAGAZINE
Programmes, September 25 - October 1, 1999
Price: £1 (Inc. VAT) €1.27

**Charlie's Angel**

**One True Love...**

**Tragedy in BallyK**

**EXCLUSIVE INTERVIEW Sting**
"LOVE! EGO! CASH!"

FINAL CLASH

**Seán Boylan & Larry Tompkins**
**AT HOME AND ON THE BALL**

MUSIC WEEK PROMOTIONAL SUPPLEMENT

release

With You In Mind, Charlie Landsborough's third album, boasts a brand new batch of 11 originals plus one very famous cover – The Isle Of Inisfree. The level of pre-orders in Britain has been exceptional and the album has just gone straight to the top of the Irish charts.

ritz artists

## Charlie Landsborough

Liverpool-based singer/songwriter Charlie was undoubtedly Ritz Records success story of 1996.

In January that year, he rocketed to overnight superstardom after just one appearance on RTE's prime time Kenny Live television show.

It was all down to a single song, the affecting What Colour Is The Wind. The title track of Charlie's second Ritz album captured the Irish imagination and sparked what host Pat Kenny termed "the greatest response ever" from any guest appearance on his show.

As a result, the album knocked Garth Brooks off the number one slot on the Irish

charts, held both Celine Dion and Riverdance at bay for five weeks and to date has sold more than 150,000 units. Final proof of his talents come with two sell-out tours of Ireland including four nights at Dublin's prestigious Gaiety Theatre, where the Live In Concert video was recorded.

The long-awaited follow-up album – With You In Mind, released in late September – will be promoted by an autumn tour which will see him accompanied by his producer and musical director Terry Bradford. The tour and release are set to establish Landsborough as a major artist in Britain as well as Ireland. The key may well be television exposure, where the former school teacher has

already proved himself capable of communicating directly with his audience.

Following a choir-augmented performance of last year's Christmas single, My Forever Friend, on BBC1's Pebble Mill, the BBC's switchboard was jammed with more than 500 calls. It was "the biggest reaction for any artist in the last series," according to BBC sources.

"Going on past sales we have no doubt Charlie will be a major success," says sales manager Yvonne Clerkin. "He just needs that one big TV appearance, as happened in Ireland, to break him to a mass audience. He's already getting a great reception concertwise, so it can only be a matter of time."

TOP 10 ALBUMS IRELAND
compiled by GALLUP
2 October 1996

1  WITH YOU IN MIND
   Charlie Landsborough
2  BLUNT
3  GRAVITY'S TONGUE
4  Trisha Yearwood
5  DAVIES LITTLE HILL
   Gloria Estefan
6  SPICE
7  THE SCORE
8  Tina Turner
9  TRAVELLING WITHOUT MOVING Jamiroquai
10 NOW THAT'S WHAT I LIKE

Cover star: Making headlines in the Irish media

The tide is turning: My record of 'Becoming an over night success'

**1995**

Thursday 19
Week 3 · 19-346

Friday 20
Week 3 · 20-345

No 2 in the Album Charts
IRELAND!

Can't believe it!
Wake me when it's over.
THANKS LORD.

Saturday 21
Week 3 · 21-344

Sunday 22
Week 3 · 22-343

Thursday 12
Week 2 · 12-353

Friday 13
Week 2 · 13-352

Saturday 14
Week 2 · 14-351

PAT KENNY SHOW
GREAT!

THANK YOU LORD!

Sunday 15
Week 2 · 15-350

February 1 2 3 4 5 6 7 8 9 10 11 12 13 14 15 16 17 18 19 20 21 22 23 24 25 26 27 28

# The Story so far....

Under Blue Skies
(CD)

The Storyteller
(CD)

Heart and Soul
(CD)

My Heart Would Know
(CD)

The Greatest Gift
(CD)

The Lighter Side
Comedy Album
(CD)

Smile
(CD)

Movin' On
(CD)

Once In a While
(CD)

The Very Best of
(CD)

What Colour Is The Wind/
Still Can't Say Goodbye
( DOUBLE CD)

With You In Mind/
Further Down The Road
(DOUBLE CD)

Songs From The Heart/
Live from Dublin
(DOUBLE CD)

An Evening With/
Shine Your Light
(DVD)

A Special Performance
(DVD)

## www.charlielandsborough.com